Executive Writing

American Style

A Business Writing Manual
for Foreign-Born Professionals

2ND EDITION

apocryphile press

BERKELEY, CA

Apocryphile Press

1700 Shattuck Ave #81

Berkeley, CA 94709

www.apocryphile.org

Printed in the United States of America

ISBN 1-933993-17-0

ACKNOWLEDGEMENTS

Our thanks to NATALIE GAST, our technical consultant, for her patience with our hurry up and wait* style and for her critical input. Natalie added value with her fresh approach to some sticky* usage issues. Natalie is the principal of Customized Language Skills Training in Little Falls, New Jersey, and Southeast Florida.

We thank ELLEN DIAMOND for her copyediting services in the first edition, which required eagle eyes* and resulted in excellent enhancements to the book.

We appreciate the above-and-beyond* services of KATHLEEN SCHULTZ and thank her for her insightful editorial suggestions as she typed the original edition of this manuscript.

Some of the content of this book has been adapted from a variety of DIAMOND ASSOCIATES writing courses. We thank, most of all, WRITING COURSE PARTICIPANTS who raised the questions that inspired us to write *Executive Writing, American Style*. We have read with great admiration material written in English for technical audiences by those whose first language is not English. Those writers should view the skills introduced in this book as high-gloss polish to their already fine finish.

---

hurry up and wait—haste made unnecessary because it's followed by inactivity

sticky—difficult

eagle eyes—eyes that see very clearly, more clearly than most

above-and-beyond—more than is necessary to do the job well

TABLE OF CONTENTS

INTRODUCTION

Executive Writing, American Style is for those of you who have mastered the English language — speaking fluently, writing intelligibly — but are not satisfied that your writing reflects precise American business writing. Whatever your profession, *Executive Writing* will help you polish your written product.

Executive Writing, American Style teaches American styles and techniques that you may choose to emulate (and also addresses those you should choose *not* to emulate). Examples cross a variety of disciplines: science, engineering, banking, technology, and general business. Practice exercises focus both on high-level editing skills (cutting excessive words and choosing appropriate ones, using American idioms correctly, mastering sentence syntax) and on the troublesome basics (verb use, pronouns, prepositions, articles, spelling, and punctuation).

Those of you using this book face two potential problems. First, you are translating the words and phrases from your language to suit your English business writing needs. In addition, you are probably following less-than-clear English business writing models from your files at work. Mastering a foreign language is difficult. Mastering a foreign language while determining which written models to follow is an extraordinary challenge. This book seeks to help you meet that challenge.

USES FOR THIS BOOK

Executive Writing, American Style is designed to aid those who prefer self-study as well as those refining their English writing through classes — in corporate training, in adult school, or in college or university settings.

SPECIAL FEATURES

Write as You Read

You will have an opportunity, as you read, to take a document from outline through edit so that you are putting to immediate use new skills and knowledge to ensure a deeper understanding of the process. The exercises are designed to help you increase the effectiveness of written documents, learn the finer points of American style and grammar, and even overcome writer's block.

From Your Files

Another way that *Executive Writing, American Style* keeps that process personalized is with prompts that allow you to use skills, as you learn, on your own documents. While practices are provided throughout the book, it is important to practice, as well, on documents that have direct relevance to your work.

Idioms Throughout

Some American idioms can be explained while for others, the best we can say is—as we titled our idiom's section— "It's just the way we say it!" Idioms are everywhere and native American speakers often don't even realize when we use them. One special feature of this book is that you will find idioms sprinkled throughout. Each is marked by an asterisk and footnoted.

As you learn idioms throughout this book, ask those around you to define others you hear. Even someone with very strong American language skills can feel at sea* when many of these expressions feel unfamiliar.

---

at sea—lost, confused, "ungrounded" as if floating at sea

Writing—A Process

-

Writing is work—hard work. It's the writer's job to make the information clear to the reader. The more you, the writer, work, the less the reader has to work. If you do a good job as a writer, your reader will appreciate it. If you are rushed or unfocused, you can be sure your reader will notice that, too. "What is written without effort is, in general, read without pleasure," observed 18th century writer, Samuel Johnson.

The Elements of Style, written by two masters of clear and concise writing, William Strunk and E.B. White, offers the following advice:

> *The purpose of good writing is not only to make oneself understood, it is to make oneself incapable of being misunderstood.*
>
> *Vigorous writing is concise. A sentence should contain no unnecessary words, a paragraph no unnecessary sentences, for the same reason that a drawing should have no unnecessary lines and a machine no unnecessary parts. This requires not that the writer make all his sentences short, or that he avoid all detail and treat his subjects only in outline, but that every word tell.*

The writing process is the same for a writer in any language. We include process in this book to give your writing a focus and a framework. We also encourage you to put your writing tasks on a timeline that works well with your other job responsibilities. Writing should fit into your schedule, but you must open the schedule enough to allow adequate time.

FOCUS

This chapter focuses on the big picture* first, rather than on details such as grammar, usage, and language. The two key elements of any written work are its audience and its purpose. The experienced writer considers these elements *before* writing. Understanding who your reader is and why you are writing gives you direction. Your style and content should vary according to audience and purpose.

One way to focus your writing is to use a tool like Jump Start* on page 6 to help you identify audience, purpose, and key points for a specific writing task. You may believe that you know these things when you sit down to write, but not be focusing on content the way your reader will. By first clarifying audience and purpose for yourself, you will have established and can maintain a clear direction as you write.

First, imagine a specific writing assignment (or select a project you are about to start): a memo, a report, a letter. As you read the following pages, complete the Jump Start page as directed.

AUDIENCE

To whom, exactly, are you writing? How much do they know? What are their questions and concerns? Just as effective speakers know their audiences, so must effective writers. Knowing your audience helps you select appropriate information and omit unnecessary details. It also helps you select the right style and tone for your writing. Most audiences want a clear, concise statement of facts and conclusions or

---

big picture—a broad overview of the subject

jump start—to give a push or a start; reference comes from "jump starting" cars (with *jumper* cables)

recommendations. They do not appreciate searching through dense paragraphs for key points.

Whether you are an engineer, a computer programmer, or an artistic director, you and the colleagues in your field have developed a language of your own. It is your jargon, your verbal shorthand. When you write to one another, you save time by using technical shorthand expressions. But remember that those outside your discipline might not speak your job language. When you write to "outsiders," you must speak a language they will understand.

Turn to Jump Start on page 6 and write a brief description of your intended audience (readers).

PURPOSE

Purpose dictates content. What, exactly, do you hope to accomplish with your document? Are you confirming a meeting? Are you requesting money for your department's budget? Are you thanking a client? You want to give the right *amount* of information—not too much and not too little. You want to give the right *kind* of information. What information must you include to accomplish your purpose with this audience?

Return to Jump Start on page 6 and write a single, clear statement of your purpose for writing this document.

KEY POINT

Now, think about your message. What is your key point? Determine the most important thing you have to say and reduce it to a single sentence.

Write your sentence on the Jump Start page.

SUPPORTING DETAILS

Finally, select relevant details that will be meaningful to your audience. For example, most members of a capital committee who determine whether to approve capital expenses do not care how many nails will be used to build a facility; they *do* care about the benefits to the company and the long-term financial projections. They care about the bottom line.*

Use the Jump Start form on page 6 to develop a short list of important facts, figures, or explanations.

If you plunge into* writing without clarifying audience, purpose, key points, and relevant supporting details, you will spend too much time editing, deleting, and rewriting.

Complete the rest of Jump Start on page 6 to establish a clear direction for your writing.

---

bottom line—the end result—In a financial balance sheet, the final total is the bottom line.

plunge into—to jump in quickly, without preparation

Use this page to focus your writing, following the directions throughout pages 4 and 5.

JUMP START

Jump start your writing by identifying:

1. Audience

2. Purpose

3. Key point

4. Supporting Details

🖥️ IT'S YOUR TURN

EXERCISE I

Now use the Jump Start form on page 8 to determine what to include in a short report (one or two paragraphs) in response to the following e-mail. The message does not include all of the information that will be critical to the report. You will have to be creative in filling in some of the Jump Start answers.

Subject: Quality Improvement Drive

Although you and I know that our quality improvement initiative is succeeding at the support staff level, I continue to receive questions from upper management about the program's success.

Can you draft something for me to send upstairs to put their minds at ease?

Thanks,
Janet

FROM YOUR FILES 📂 The next time you have a writing project, start with a Jump Start summary that defines your specific audience and purpose.

JUMP START

Use this form to complete Exercise 1.

1. AUDIENCE *(brief description of your intended audience)*

2. PURPOSE *(a single, clear statement of your purpose for writing this document)*

3. KEY POINT *(your most important point)*

4. SUPPORTING DETAILS *(supporting information)*

STEPS TO GOOD WRITING

The tried and true writing process includes six steps:
Plan, Outline, Draft, Edit, Rewrite, Proofread. The writing
process doesn't always follow neatly progressive steps, but
it *must* begin with a plan. Then, you have choices. Some
people outline first; some write the draft. You may start with
either, but must include both.

PLAN

Plan first. Planning to write requires thinking about your
audience and purpose, gathering necessary information, and
reviewing appropriate resources. Plan your time and your
place to write. Try to create an environment in which you
can focus. Research facts, figures, and missing details first
so that your draft can flow without interruption.

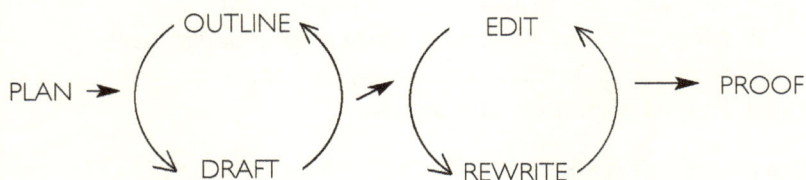

OUTLINE

One common method of organizing thoughts is an outline.
The outline helps you get your act together.* You may
develop a formal outline with Roman numerals, numbers,
upper- and lower-case letters, and more. Other options are
a more casual—or topic—outline and a brainstorm outline.
Example 1 is a **formal outline** for a proposal for funds to
renovate and expand a facility.

---

get your act together—to get organized

EXAMPLE 1: FORMAL OUTLINE

PROPOSAL

I. BACKGROUND
   A. Facility built in 1968
   B. Had been used to house one department of 20 people
   C. Department has expanded to 65 people

II. PRESENT CONDITIONS
   A. Overcrowded offices
   B. Inadequate electrical capacity
   C. Inadequate parking

III. PROPOSED ACTION
   A. Renovate and expand internal space
   B. Upgrade electrical capacity
   C. Expand parking lot

IV. POTENTIAL BENEFITS
   A. Adequate workspace for each department
   B. More efficient work within and among departments
   C. Space to accommodate new equipment
   D. Improved parking conditions

V. ALTERNATIVES
   A. Find new space in other buildings
   B. Build new facility
   C. Postpone any action for one to two years

Naturally, your outline does not need to be this formal (or this detailed); it should be a personal tool to help you plan the writing. Any outline you use should fit your own preference.

One flexible approach is the **topic outline.** As you put words on paper, do not translate. Use words that come easily, letting your thoughts flow from mind to page in whatever language they occur. Translating comes later, as does editing.

EXAMPLE 2: TOPIC OUTLINE

PROPOSAL

Introduction
    – general overview
Background
    – *histoire*
    – *raisonnement*
Current Conditions
    – electric
    – autopark
    – office space
Advantages/Benefits
    – staff in more logical space
    – offices get state-of-the art equipment
    – better client impression/image
    – more $
    – profit long-run?
    – *quand?*
    – *combien?*
Alternatives
    – move
    – find shared space in next building
    – *rien*

Often, writers do not have their thoughts organized thorough-ly enough to develop a linear outline first. One creative out-lining option is known as the **brainstorm outline,** or map-ping. In mapping, the writer puts all ideas on paper rapidly in random order (and random placement on the page), jotting down ideas as they come to mind and ignoring spelling and structure. Then, the writer reviews all topics, deletes some, and organizes those that are relevant. This is similar to the brainstorming process used in meetings: all thoughts are accepted; none are rejected. The group (or, in this case, the writer) later selects the best ideas.

EXAMPLE 3: BRAINSTORM OUTLINE (MAPPING)
Notice that capitalization and structure are not consistent.
This is a working outline.

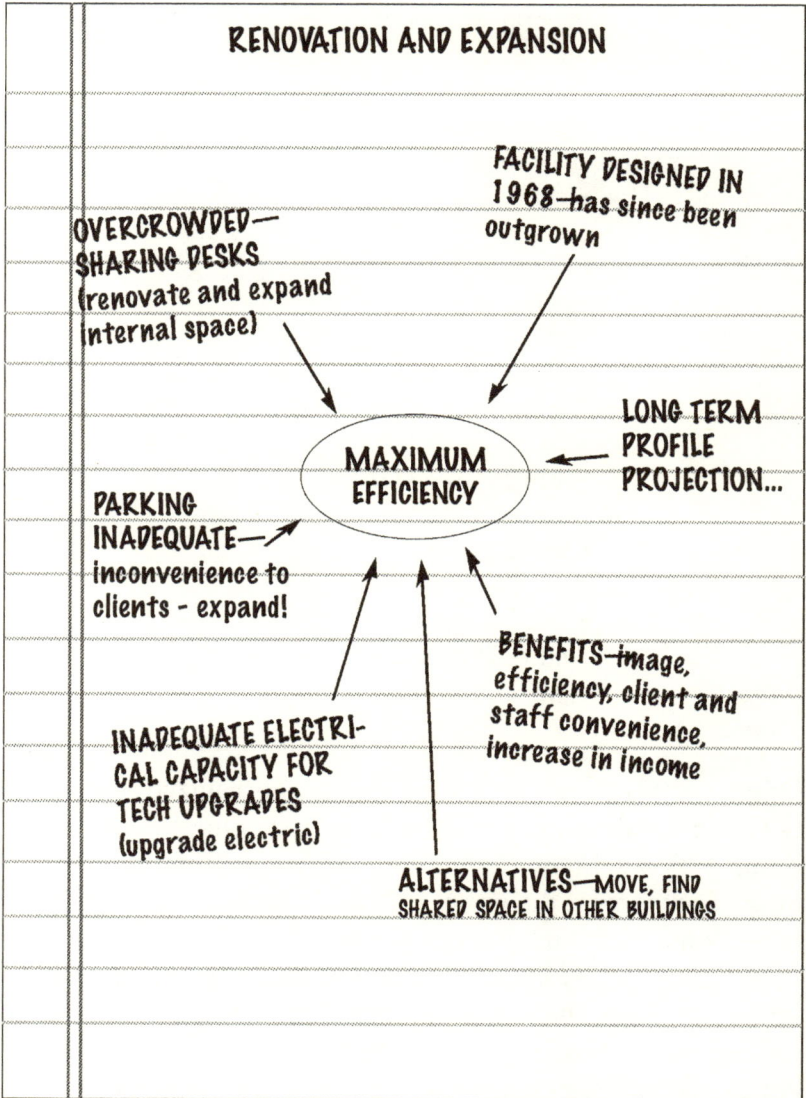

RENOVATION AND EXPANSION

FACILITY DESIGNED IN 1968—has since been outgrown

OVERCROWDED—SHARING DESKS (renovate and expand internal space)

LONG TERM PROFILE PROJECTION...

MAXIMUM EFFICIENCY

PARKING INADEQUATE—inconvenience to clients - expand!

BENEFITS—image, efficiency, client and staff convenience, increase in income

INADEQUATE ELECTRICAL CAPACITY FOR TECH UPGRADES (upgrade electric)

ALTERNATIVES—MOVE, FIND SHARED SPACE IN OTHER BUILDINGS

⌨ IT'S YOUR TURN

EXERCISE 2

Select one of the following topics and develop an outline, using any of the forms discussed: formal, topic, or brainstorm.

☙   A recommendation to reorganize your department or division

☙   A request for $4 million to renovate an outdated laboratory

☙   A report on a conference you attended that focused on family issues in business

FROM YOUR FILES 🗁   (1) Develop an outline for a writing project you are about to start.   (2) Analyze a successful report or proposal and construct a brief topic outline to show how the writer organized content.

DRAFT

Some writers prefer to first "dump" all their thoughts (in sentence and paragraph form) on paper or on the computer, then delete and organize later. A real rough draft is the product of the dump draft approach.

Once you complete the dump draft, you have to review it and organize the thoughts that tumbled out in random order. You cannot go directly to editing; you must reorder (almost outline) that draft.

SAMPLE DUMP DRAFT

RENOVATION/EXPANSION

Present facility is inadequate—lacks office space (the personnel department can't even interview in comfort, and the marketing support staff is sharing desk space and doesn't have room—or electrical capability—to buy the kind of equipment that would keep the operation up-to-date and running smoothly). Also there are too many people working in building for the autopark. We walk a long way and clients don't know how to find the office. Building built in 1968 and looks it—bad impression, more serious is effect on organization and productivity. Could, perhaps, hold on for a few years, could beg space from building next door, need to find right group—time—alternative. [check budget current and projected]

Current conditions (fill in details)
-
-
-

Proposed conditions (fill in details)
-
-
-

Our proposal [adequately, easily, sufficiently] answers several corporate objectives:
(list)

Identify the "starting point" that works best for you. Now that you have a skeleton from which to work, it is time to put meat on the bones. As you write the draft, you must control the urge to edit. Do not stop to check spelling, punctuation, facts, and figures, or word choice. If words or phrases from your fist language come to mind more easily than English words, pepper* the draft with them. Editing while you write will clog your creative pipeline.* Just go with the flow.*

🖥 IT'S YOUR TURN

EXERCISE 3

Use either the Jump Start format (see page 6) or one of the outlines (pages 10-12) as your base and develop the first two paragraphs of your draft.

EDIT

The next step, editing, is difficult. After you have worked hard to put words on paper, you may be reluctant to change—or worse, delete—them. Now is the time to slow down and find the right word, the correct punctuation, and the sentence structure that works best. For a writer whose first language is not English, this process might include translating words tossed into your first draft from your first language. For any writer, this process involves searching for the right word. Remember, save the editing job for the end; do not edit as you write. Writing and editing are two distinct processes.

If possible, edit after you have taken a break from your writing. Break for a few days if you can, or for only a few hours if you have little time. Every time you return to a written piece, you will see something you did not see before. To edit, use the following checklists and employ the techniques you will learn as you use this book. Chapter 8 offers more detailed editing practice.

---

*pepper—to sprinkle throughout
*clog the pipeline—to slow things down
*go with the flow—to take things as they come

ESL/GRAMMAR CHECKLIST ☑

correct verb endings	(Chapters 5 & 6)
correct and consistent pronouns	(Chapter 3)
consistent and precise tense	(Chapter 6)
appropriate prepositions	(Chapter 3)
only necessary adjectives	(Chapter 4)
correctly placed modifiers	(Chapter 4)
correct word order in questions	(Chapter 4)
the best verbs (action words)	(Chapter 4)
the most precise nouns	(Chapter 4)
phrases close to words they modify	(Chapter 4)
articles when necessary	(Chapter 3)
correct possessives and plurals	(Chapter 4)
appropriate tone (not too formal, not too informal)	(Chapter 2)
subject/verb agreement	(Chapter 4)
verb tense	(Chapters 5 & 6)
parallel construction	(Chapter 4)

EDITOR'S CHECKLIST ✔

Content:
- Accurate
- Clear
- Concise
- Correct (grammar, punctuation, spelling)

Format:
- Title is concrete and descriptive.
- Format follows company guidelines.
- Format is consistent.
- Subheads break text.
- Graphs, drawings, tables, other visuals support text.

Structure:
- Each section:
  - contains only information pertinent to the section.
  - uses clear, logical sentences.
- Each paragraph:
  - uses meaningful transitions.
  - has most sentences in active voice.
- Each sentence contains:
  - an average of 15 to 20 words.
  - a limited number of prepositional phrases.
  - clear terminology.
  - no excess.
  - no more than two or three connected ideas.

Order and Sequence:
- An Executive Summary or Abstract or strong first paragraph summarizes the main point up front.
- Ideas flow logically.
- The structural "roadmap" is obvious.
- Cross references within the document are consistent, correct, and clear.

Reference Material:
- A good English dictionary (on the shelf or online)
- A good [your language]/English dictionary (on the shelf or online)
- A good thesaurus (on the shelf or online)
- Spell-checker
- Grammar-checker

🖳 IT'S YOUR TURN

EXERCISE 4

1. Edit the draft you wrote for Exercise 3. Then, look at the edited draft for Exercise 3 in the Answer Key.

FROM YOUR FILES 📁 Select the item from your files for which you used either Jump Start *or* Draft and then edit the first three paragraphs. Use the checklists on the preceding pages as your guide.

REWRITE

After you edit, you must review your entire letter, memo, report, or proposal for consistency. Did some changes require others that you may have overlooked? Review and rewrite where necessary to ensure clarity and consistency.

PROOF

Proofreading is a critical step before you let your writing go public.* Small mistakes—misspellings, incorrect punctuation, missing words, inaccurate figures—can cause major problems and detract from your professional image.

Proofreading, like writing, should be done in stages for maximum effect.

---

* *go public*—to be seen by others (From stock market language—A private company *goes public* when it sells stock to the open market.)

Proofreading 1-2-3:

1. Read through for content.
   - Does it make sense?
   - Do thoughts follow one another logically?

2. Read slowly, pointing to each word to ensure accuracy.
   - Are words spelled correctly?
   - Is grammar correct?

3. Have someone else proofread your work. Discuss any points with which you do not agree before you decide to incorporate his or her corrections.

IT'S YOUR TURN

EXERCISE 5

Rewrite the paragraphs you wrote and edited. Do they need some rewriting? Use the Editor's Checklist. Make necessary changes. Now, proofread your work.

EXERCISE 1

Answers will vary from person to person. Here is a possible answer, based on the Jump Start.

1. **AUDIENCE** (reader): Top Management

2. **PURPOSE** (writer's purpose): To assure success of quality initiative at support staff level

3. **KEY POINT** (in one clear sentence): Support level staff members have demonstrated, through changes in behavior and procedures, their understanding and acceptance of the quality initiative's customer service focus.

4. **SUPPORTING DETAILS:**
   Specific examples of procedure and behavior changes
   Specific benefits (customer related) of these changes
   How we learned about the specific benefits

EXERCISE 2

Sample Topic Outline
The Marketing Department's Reorganization Plan

Background
   - During the past six years, the marketing department has doubled its staff and tripled its workload.
   - Two of every five employees is in a management position.
   - Other departments complain about slow turnaround time.
   - The marketing staff barely keeps up with work demands.

Proposed Reorganization
   - Develop marketing teams of three or four people to serve designated client departments.
   - Maintain a circular review loop.
   - Establish clear time frames for projects and communicate them to all client departments.
   - Establish alternative plans for unexpected delays.

Benefits
- More staff will be available to keep workflow moving.
- Client departments will establish ongoing relationships, limiting the learning curve.*
- Contingency plans and people will be available.

Sample Brainstorm Outline—First Dump Draft
Request for $4 Million to Renovate Research Laboratory

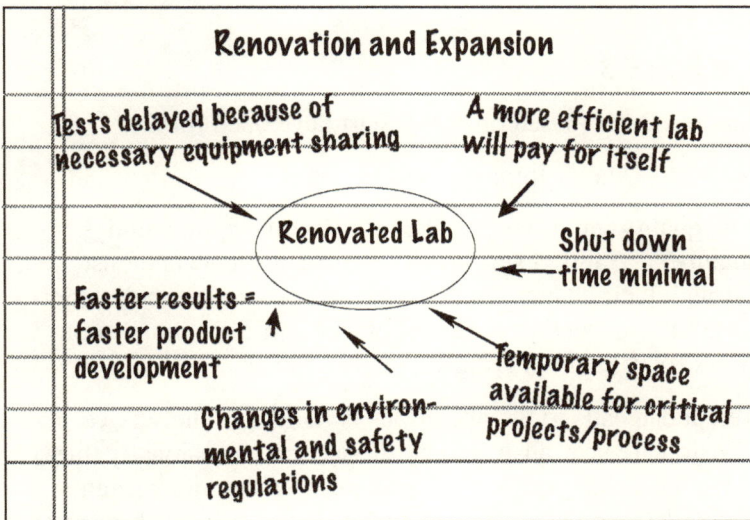

Sample Formal Outline: *Family Issues in Business Forum*

I. Conference Details
    A. Place, date, name
    B. Key forms

II. Workshops
    A. Health Care Track
    B. Child Care Track
    C. Wellness Track
    D. Open Forum

---

* *learning curve*—the time it takes someone to learn something

III. Keynote Speaker
   A. Dinner Tues.
   B. Luncheon Wed.
   C. Closing Wed.

IV. Actions to Table
   A. Write to legislators.
   B. Talk with HR about implementing a childcare program.
   C. Suggest speaking at next conference about company's wellness program.

EXERCISE 3

Sample Draft (based on Jump Start developed for Ex. 1)

Subject: Quality Improvement Initiative

The quality initiative has taken root* with support staff members. Support staff in all departments have demonstrated, through their changes in behavior and procedure, their under-standing—as well as their acceptance—of the quality initia-tive's focus on improving customer service.

Telephone calls to the operations division and the service division are now answered by the second (occasionally third) ring. This change alone has generated verbal and written accolades from customers and employees. A walk through any department shows with clarity our quality improvement.

⊙ _____

*take root—to be solid; to develop a strong position

2

Writing, American Style

- ✍ TAKING THE "CHARM" OUT OF THE BUSINESS LETTER
- ✍ THE SIMPLE, DIRECT APPROACH
- ✍ BUSINESSESE DINOSAURS
- ✍ ABSTRACT LANGUAGE = VAGUE MESSAGE
- ✍ CONCRETE LANGUAGE = OBJECTIVE APPRAISAL

TAKING THE "CHARM" OUT OF THE BUSINESS LETTER

The following letter would bring a smile of pleasure to a banker's Indian client, but would sound strange to that client's American counterpart.

> Dear Rajani:
>
> Our bank conveys its most sincere appreciation for your valued and excellent association. From the humble origins of your business, during the years of its inspirational growth, continuing during its laudable and enviable success today, we have been honored to serve you. Midtown Bank offers its most enthusiastic congratulations on your business expansion.

The American business writing style may be short on charm but is highly effective in its direct, confident approach. It's a style that meets the basic requirements of today's busy executives: factual, concise, and relevant. Those who read and write business communications in this fast-paced business climate do not have the luxury of time. Charm, therefore, is less valued than brevity in our Western culture, and direct, spare* writing sounds authoritative, strong, and believable to most North Americans.

Consider the differing tones of these requests.

I. As you and your esteemed colleagues are well aware, Brand X has unfortunately and unexpectedly adversely affected our quite excellent sales results in the Western region. We, therefore, request your kind consideration of our proposal to focus all serious attention upon our recent research and development successes in upgrading our own Brand Z in order that we may potentially compete with a more improved product.

---

*spare—to the point; without excess; cut to the bone

II. During the fourth quarter of 2006, Brand X unexpectedly captured 5 percent of our 60 percent market share in the Western region. We propose immediately implementing Research and Development's new product improvements to Brand Z. With an upgraded product, we can effectively counter Brand X's inroads into the Western market.

In Sample II, the American business version, the gracious phrases have been replaced with factual information. Only a few important modifiers are used: u*nexpectedly, immediately, new, upgraded, effectively.* They give information needed to understand the request.

Sample II also uses precise verbs (*captured, counter*) and nouns (*market share, inroads*) instead of depending on adjectives. In Sample I, many more modifiers are used, most of which are not necessary to the meaning of the proposal: *esteemed, well, unfortunately, unexpectedly, adversely, quite, excellent, kind, all, serious, recent, potentially, more, improved.*

In addition, some of Sample I's modifiers were replaced in Sample II with factual data: a*dversely affected our quite excellent results* was replaced by *captured 5 percent of our 60 percent market share.*

U.S. managers always favor hard* information over general phrases, no matter how smoothly the generalities flow. The statement of facts allows the managers to form their own impressions of the information, and they'll thank you for the opportunity to do so. Any serious manager would expect you to provide data to support your personal opinions or general descriptions. Why not write the factual sentence in the first place?

Another important point is that in Sample II any modifiers (*esteemed, well, kind, all, serious*) that describe the reader or the writer have been omitted because flattery is suspect in the American style. Readers wonder whether the writer is buttering

---

hard—specific; factual

them up* before lowering the boom.* Complimentary phrase-ology from a more gracious age or more gracious part of the world is out of place in modern American business writing.

Finally, choosing the best single modifier, rather than stacking up a list of lesser ones is a hallmark* of good writing style. In place of Sample I's *recent research and development successes in upgrading our own Brand Z...a more improved product,* the American business writer used *Research and Development's new product improvements...upgraded product...*

The American preference for a strong statement rather than a polite request is especially evident in the closing sentence: *With an upgraded product, we can effectively counter Brand X's inroads into the Western market,* which replaced Sample I's *We, therefore, request your kind consideration of our proposal to focus all serious...that we may potentially compete with a more improved product.*

Cutting the charming—but unnecessary—modifiers changes the tone of the summary. It also shortens the paragraph, satisfying two important guidelines of good business writing style: (a) be concise and (b) include only relevant content. The resulting tone is pure, confident American style.

A few simple guidelines can help you keep your writing relevant and concise.

☞ Write only **when you must**, not when you don't have to.

☞ Write only **what you must**; no filler phrases.

---

butter up—to try to gain approval by flattery
lower the boom—to give bad news without warning
hallmark—a distinguishing feature; a symbol of quality

🖳 IT'S YOUR TURN

Exercise 1

Select concrete, direct words and phrases to replace the polite and charming fillers.

POLITE FILLERS	DIRECT WORDS & PHRASES
1. I thank you for your kind response.	
2. Please be advised that your loan has been approved.	
3. We eagerly await your reply.	
4. Thanking you in advance for your cooperation.	
5. Our excellent client...	
6. It is in the realm of possibility that...	
7. Be so kind as to send...	

🖳 IT'S YOUR TURN

Exercise 2

Rewrite the letter to Rajani, which begins this chapter, in a less charming, more direct style.

THE SIMPLE, DIRECT APPROACH

American business people are not unfriendly or insensitive; they are focused on the job. That focus can work in your interest if you send the kind of tightly-written* message the reader can process quickly. How would you to simplify and tighten this request?

> We respectfully request that you kindly review your files and advise us, upon your review, of the correct recipient of this interest payment.

Try it:

_____

_____

Did you consider these steps?

☞ First, cut polite fillers and use the simplest request format possible:

We respectfully request that you kindly should be replaced by the stronger, equally polite substitute *please*.

☞ Next, be careful about other excess phrases:

Upon your review is redundant. The reader has already been asked to review the files and it is obvious that a response providing the requested information would follow that review.

The message should be rewritten this way:

Please
~~We respectfully request that you kindly~~ ∧ review your files and ~~urgent~~ly advise us, ~~upon your review,~~ of the correct recipient of this interest payment.

---

tightly written—written with no excess words

IT'S YOUR TURN

EXERCISE 3

Edit the following e-mail to a pharmaceutical company's packaging department, removing the charming phrases and using direct language to make important points.

Subject: Extraneous material and semi-finished product problems during packaging

During the months of February and March, all of you have very determinedly and aggressively packaged several batches, only to find out that unfortunately some of the packaged goods need to be opened for extraneous materials. You in the Packaging Department will no doubt have to laboriously unpack approximately 100,000 units. It is certainly critical that we discuss these crucial concerns with our responsible associates and request input from all to solve these problems. Therefore, as soon as possible, I will arrange a department meeting to examine these issues.

I thank and admire our esteemed associates who found these problems in their groups. However, can you imagine if a packaged bottle or a blister reaches a consumer with a foreign tablet or capsule in it? Our reputed company would suffer drastic consequences such as immediate recall, an FDA inspection, and loss of credibility as pharmaceutical professionals.

BUSINESSESE DINOSAURS

Don't follow the wrong models! On your way to good, clear American style, there's more to cut than unnecessary charm. Remember, the letters and memos you receive from American-born writers may not provide the best models. While the American business writing style may not be charming, it is often inflated and wordy. Many words and phrases are business-writing "dinosaurs"—outdated terms that can be replaced by shorter or fewer words—or simply deleted. The legal profession has had a strong influence on business writing, but even American lawyers now make an effort to simplify their writing and make it reader-friendly.* The words and phrases in Exercise 4 are examples of dinosaurs.

IT'S YOUR TURN

EXERCISE 4

For the words and phrases in the first column, write a more direct, natural phrase (or a single-word replacement) in the second column. The first seven are done for you.

Instead of:	**Use:**
1. We regret to inform you	_We regret that_ or _We're sorry that_
2. In the event that	_If_
3. A review of the aforementioned figures appears to reveal	_A review shows_ or _The figures reveal_
4. Had occasion to be	_Was_
5. In order to	_To; (To review)_
6. In order that	_So (that)_
7. It is often the case that	_Often; Occasionally_

*reader-friendly—easy to read

	Instead of:	**Use:**
8.	In the amount of	_____
9.	Due to the fact that	_____
10.	At a later date	_____
11.	As per your letter	_____
12.	Eliminate altogether	_____
13.	Hopefully, you will agree that	_____
14.	Reach an agreement	_____
16.	Without further delay	_____
17.	Make an acquisition	_____
18.	For the purpose of reviewing	_____
19.	For the purpose of	_____
20.	In a position to	_____
21.	In a number of cases	_____
22.	In connection with	_____
23.	It is apparent that	_____
24.	It is clear that	_____
25.	Please note that	_____
26.	On a daily basis	_____
27.	On behalf of	_____
28.	Place a major emphasis on	_____
29.	Referred to as	_____
31.	Through the use of	_____
32.	We wish to	_____
34.	With the result that	_____
35.	Within the realm of possibility	_____
36.	It is necessary to note	_____

🖳 IT'S YOUR TURN

EXERCISE 5

Practice conveying your meaning with brevity. In fact, one English word can replace all of these phrases. What is it?

approximately	pursuant to	in reference to
relative to	in relation to	regarding
in the matter of	respecting	in connection about
the matter of	in the range of	in the vicinity of
more or less	with regard to	on the order of
with respect to	on the subject of	in the ballpark*

FROM YOUR FILES 🗁 Find a letter or e-mail written by a foreign-born writer (perhaps your own letter) and find one written by an American. In both, remove all the charming words, unnecessary modifiers, and stiff businessese phrases. Probably the two samples have much in common—much to cut!

ABSTRACT LANGUAGE = VAGUE MESSAGE

Once you cut "soft" words, charming fillers, and businessese— your writing will begin to look spare, perhaps too spare. As you select words to build your message, remember the advice that "every word tell." Choose words that speak to your readers and answer their question with concrete, specific information.

Abstract words such as *valuable*, *acceptable*, and *beneficial* come easily because they are vague and general. The reader is left with the questions "What makes this valuable, acceptable, beneficial?" To replace abstract words with concrete, ask yourself **who, what, when, where, why, and how**? These are known as the typical reporter questions;* they elicit facts.

---

*in the ballpark—(from baseball) in the vicinity of

*reporter questions—the standard questions asked by reporters

🖳 IT'S YOUR TURN

EXERCISE 6

The following sentences rely on **abstract** words (shown in italics). Provide concrete information to replace these words. The first sentence is done for you. Remember, if a reader would have to ask the reporter questions, your writing is not concrete.

1. The Travel Authority plans to make interstate travel *more efficient*.

    <u>Correction</u> *The Travel Authority plans to to improve interstate travel by adding two bus lines and increasing rush hour train service from every half-hour to every fifteen minutes.* (These sentence answers the question, "**How** does the Travel Authority plan to make interstate travel more efficient?")

2. Our requisition approval process is *cumbersome*.

3. The company's health benefit program is *effective*.

4. The new software is a *valuable* resource.

EXERCISE 7

Rewrite the following statement using more precise words to answer the reader's questions.

Our department is planning to install a valuable new software program to work with your accounting program; the change will benefit the company financially.

↳ *planning to install* **When**? **Whom** will be affected? **How**?

↳ *valuable* **How**? **What** does it do?

↳ *benefit the company financially* **How**?

CONCRETE LANGUAGE = OBJECTIVE APPRAISAL

Word choice is critical when a manager writes performance evaluations and appraisals. Abstract words are subjective and evaluative and can cause emotional reactions; concrete words are descriptive, giving work-related facts that must be examined objectively.

If you tell an employee that he or she is uncooperative or unreliable, that employee should rightfully ask, "What did I **do** that would make you call me that?" Rather than having to address the negative emotions and defensive behavior that charged* words like *uncooperative* and *unreliable* will elicit, use concrete language. You can then focus on the work-related behavior you want to change. Often, criticism given correctly can turn a diamond in the rough* into a gem.*

Positive words can leave doubt, too. Excellent workers want to know exactly what behaviors led to their excellent evaluations, so they can continue them. Concrete language on evaluations is especially important because words like "excellent worker" are too subjective and vague to help someone looking through the files for specific strengths, skills, or levels of initiative.

Being specific in your praise is motivational. It shows that you recognize and appreciate particular efforts and contributions.

---

charged—conveying emotion, like an electrical charge
diamond in the rough—someone with unused potential
gem—a jewel; in this context, a valued and valuable employee

IT'S YOUR TURN

EXERCISE 8

The following words might appear on an employee's performance appraisal. Write a specific behavior or action that is a
concrete example of each evaluative word or phrase.

1. uncooperative _____

_____

2. has an attitude problem _____

_____

3. excellent worker_____

_____

4. careless_____

_____

5. dependable _____

_____

6. time-waster_____

_____

EXERCISE 9

Write a summary paragraph for an appraisal of an employee you
might be supervising. (If you do not supervise, select someone
you wish you could appraise.) First, brainstorm a list of
abstract words that describe this employee. Then think of concrete examples to support each abstract word. Use the concrete
examples in your summary.

A
N
S
W
E
R

K
E
Y

EXERCISE 1

1. Thank you for your response.
2. Your loan has been approved.
   or Central Bank has approved your loan.
3. Please reply by (*date*).
4. Thank you for your cooperation.
5. Our valued client... *or* Our client...
6. Perhaps...
7. Please send...

EXERCISE 2

Individual answers will differ. Did you eliminate unnecessary words and phrases? Here is one possible answer:

Dear Rajani:

Congratulations on your business expansion. Midtown Bank is delighted to have been able to meet your start-up banking needs and to continue to serve you during these exciting times of growth.

EXERCISE 3

E-mail Revision:

During February and March, we efficiently packaged several batches and then discovered that some of the packaged goods contained extraneous material. The Packaging Department will have to unpack approximately 100,000 units.

I congratulate those who found these problems in their groups, enabling us to correct them before sending out the product. Fortunately, we avoided the serious consequences of immediate recall, an FDA inspection, and loss of professional credibility.

To prevent such problems in the future, we must review this incident. I will, therefore, arrange a full department meeting as soon as possible.

EXERCISE 4

8	For	22.	With
9.	Because	23.	Apparently
10.	Later	24.	Clearly
11.	According to your letter	25.	Note:
12.	Eliminate	26.	Daily
13.	I hope you agree that	27.	For
14.	Agree	28.	Emphasize
16.	Immediately	29.	As, Called, Named
17.	Acquire	31.	By, Through
18.	To review	32.	*Delete this phrase.*
19.	To	34.	Resulting in
20.	Can, May	35.	Possible
21.	Often, Frequently	36.	Please note

EXERCISE 5

About

EXERCISE 6

Individual answers will vary from these suggestions. If your reader would still have to ask **what, when, why, how, where,** or **how much,** your answer is not concrete.

2. Our requisition process, which requires four signatures, takes two weeks.

3. The company's health benefit program gives employees ample coverage and keeps costs within a reasonable range.

4. The new software has cut project completion time in half.

EXERCISE 7

Sample rewrite:

During the fourth quarter of 2007, our department will upgrade to AccountSuite, a new software program that will allow all invoices and general ledgers to link directly with the main ledger system. This program will decrease accounting reporting times by 30 percent.

EXERCISE 8

Individual answers will vary from the suggested answers
below. If you can still ask "What does (did) someone do to
cause him or her to be described as uncooperative (etc.)?"
your answer is not concrete.

1. *uncooperative*
   refuses to share information with the company auditor; is
   reluctant to share passwords with the entire project team

2. *has an attitude problem*
   never smiles; does not acknowledge greetings; slams
   papers down on others' desks

3. *excellent worker*
   initiates projects; asks relevant questions; writes quickly
   and effectively

4. *careless*
   does not proofread correspondence; staples pages out of
   order; does not return client phone calls

5. *dependable*
   covers others' phones; arrives at work early; is willing to
   stay late; completes projects on time and within budget

6. *time-waster*
   does not ask appropriate questions and causes work to
   wait for clarification; does not expedite phone conversa-
   tions; does not group tasks; stops to chat with coworkers
   too frequently

EXERCISE 9

Sample list of abstract words:

responsible, punctual, eager, efficient

Sample appraisal summary:

Henry is always available to assume greater responsibility.
He completes his weekly projects well within schedule and
requests additional work. I suggest sending Henry for
management training.

3

Little Words, Big Trouble

- ARTICLES: LITTLE WORDS MEAN A LOT
- PREPOSITIONS: SMALL WORDS FOR BIG CONNECTIONS
- PRONOUNS: THE RIGHT SUBSTITUTES

ARTICLES: LITTLE WORDS MEAN A LOT

Many languages do not use articles—*a, an,* and *the.* In English, however, articles are essential because they add meaning to nouns. Using articles correctly clarifies writing and helps the reader move through your sentences with ease. Sometimes, those whose first language is not English omit articles, insert them randomly, or insert them where articles are used in their native languages. In English, articles **always precede nouns**.

Sometimes articles are necessary to sentence structure.

> Sales showed *a* 23 percent increase in 2006.
> The company is *an* independent entity.
> The company's stock is traded on *the* Nasdaq.

It's a lot of attention to give three little words, referred to as "indefinite" (*a, an*) and "definite" (*the*) articles. This chapter offers guidelines to help you determine when each article is appropriate, when to include each, and when not to. Keep in mind that most nouns are defined in some way. One way is by showing that a noun is singular or plural. The other is by using determiners, which include articles.

The following examples illustrate the differences in the use of articles and the general (non-specific) or specific implications they give to nouns:

non-specific implication:
> *plural*: *Vacations* are excellent stress relievers.
> *the*:   *The vacation* is an excellent stress reliever.
> *a*:   *A vacation* is an excellent stress reliever.

specific implication:
> *the:*   *The vacation* that I took in Europe ended too soon!
> *the + plural*: *The vacations* our company awards top sales people are getting better every year.
> *a*:   Last fall I took *a vacation* to visit my sister in India.

Vacations without an article is the most general, and *the vaca -tions* is the most specific. All others can be general or specific, depending on the context. No wonder these little words are big trouble!

A Word on Context

Context refers to both the written piece and the background information of the writer and the reader. What do they already know? In what context is the information presented? We choose an article to suit the context, making the same noun general in one context and specific in another. Although *the* is usually more specific than *a*, it is not always specific. Articles don't have meaning of their own; they add meaning to nouns, and the meaning they add depends largely on context.

Definite or Indefinite?

The **definite article** (*the*) is usually specific.

statement: I need *the* book.—*The* book refers to a specific book.

The **indefinite article** (a) may indicate either a general or a specific noun; it may also be ambiguous. It is what it claims to be: indefinite. A noun with an indefinite article that is non-specific may become specific when context is added.

statement: I need *a book.*—This is ambiguous. What book?
general meaning: any book
specific meaning (in the context of a class):
                    the workbook for this class

statement: I'm looking for *a book.* What book?
general meaning: any book
specific meaning (context: I've been reading a novel):
                    the novel I was reading

Look at the following two sentences. Context determines how specific or general the nouns are in each sentence. Does the speaker know about the meeting that took place?

Did you attend a meeting on Monday?
Did you attend the meeting on Monday?

The first question is ambiguous; it could be either general or specific, depending on the context. Context #1: The speaker (writer) knows that there were department meetings throughout the company and you work with more than one department and wants to know whether you attended one of them. Context #2: The speaker has no idea what your Monday schedule was and wonders whether it included a meeting.

The second sentence would be asked only by someone who thought it possible that you had plans to attend a particular meeting.

"A" OR "AN"

For ease in pronunciation, we use *an* instead of *a* before a vowel sound. This includes most words that begin with vowels—A, E, I, O, U—among others. This pronunciation-based usage is extended to written English. Listen to the difference between *honor* and *horror*. Each begins with the same consonant, but *honor* begins with a vowel sound, while *horror* begins with a consonant sound (*H*). The same is true for words that begin with *U*. Unique and uncertain both begin with a vowel, but unique begins with a consonant sound (*Y*) and uncertain with a vowel sound. It's not what you see, it's what you hear that determines the correct indefinite article.

Remember: The difference in use between *a* and *an* is based on ease of pronunciation; its form (*a* or *an*) is determined by the word that follows it. For example: I have *an* umbrella. I have *a* blue umbrella. If you try to say *a umbrella*, you'll notice that the transition does not sound smooth. When writing, if you're not sure which indefinite article is correct, say the word aloud.

We met in *an* elevator.
They work for *a* European company.
He has *an* understanding boss.
We have *a* union.
We are meeting in *an* hour.
We are meeting in *a* half an hour.
Olga works in *an* HR department.
Olga works in *a* human resources department.

A WORD ON "THE"

Use *the* when using a noun for the second time. It is now a specific noun because you mentioned it once. You're making it more specific by giving more details.

I attended *a* meeting. *The* meeting was boring.

Conversely, after you make a specific statement, you may, if you wish, follow it with a generality.

I attended *the* boring meeting.
A meeting shouldn't be five hours long.

ARTICLES AND PROPER NOUNS

In most cases, articles are not used with proper nouns (names).

Take Joe to St. Barnabas Hospital.
but: Take Joe to *the* hospital. or Take Joe to *a* hospital.

Let's go to Summit Bank.
but: Let's go to *the* bank. or Let's go to *a* bank.

The Inevitable Exceptions:

1. Use the article before the name of the department when the word *department* is in the sentence, but do not use the article when you drop the word *department*.

   I work for *the* Engineering Department.
   I work for *an* engineering department.
   I work for Engineering.

2 Some companies have *the* as part of their names.

He is a manager at **The** Hilton.
The company president was quoted in **The** New York Times.

3 Some proper nouns have a general noun as part of their names, such as *court* and *commission*. In such cases, inject *the* before the noun phrase.

Who will be appointed to *the* Supreme Court?
She works for *the* Securities and Exchange Commission.

4 Some proper nouns have become so common that we use them as generic nouns.

Please make *a* xerox of these documents.
Do you have *a* kleenex?

(*Xerox* is commonly used to mean any photocopy, not just a Xerox copy. *Kleenex* is commonly used to mean any tissue, not just a Kleenex tissue.)

PLURALS

In the plural, we don't need an indefinite article when the meaning is general. Use of the plural *with* the definite article (*the*) gives the noun a very specific meaning.

Based on *conservative estimates*, restructuring is realistic.

Based on *a conservative estimate*, restructuring is realistic.

Based on *the conservative estimates* of XY Co. and YZ Corp., restructuring is realistic.

The first example above refers to many different estimates; the second example, to one specific estimate; and the third example, to a specific set or group of estimates. Clearly, the choice of article and use of the plural with the article affect your meaning.

Reminder: *A* can refer only to a singular noun; *the* applies to both singular and plural.

⌨ IT'S YOUR TURN

EXERCISE 1

Think about the meaning of price in each sentence below.
Indicate which are general and which are specific.

1.	Prices rose 15 percent.	general	specific
2.	The price rose 15 percent.	general	specific
3.	The prices rose 15 percent.	general	specific

⌨ IT'S YOUR TURN

EXERCISE 2

Write two sentences, the first using the general meaning of
the noun corporations (plural), the second using specific
corporations.

1. _____

2. _____

COUNT AND NON-COUNT NOUNS

The difference between "count" and "non-count" nouns is as
simple as it sounds. "Count" nouns can be counted while "non-
count" nouns are not typically counted. Some examples follow:

non count	count
money	dollars
	dimes
time	hours
	minutes
coffee	cups of coffee
air	breaths of air

Money and air would not typically be used as plurals; however time and coffee can be used as "count" nouns in specific situations: an order of "two coffees"; talk of different "times."

"Non-count" nouns can be used without being specific. For example, *science* is a non-count noun when it is used as a general term. However, "non-count" nouns are not *always* strictly "non-count." Once we use an article or a plural, the noun becomes a "count" noun, or "countable."

Notice the specific meaning that is added by articles.

> The job involves some knowledge of *science*. [non-count]
> Genetics is *a science* that is continually expanding. [count]
> Genetics is *the science* about which I know the least. [count]
> This job involves some knowledge of *the science*s. [count]

Encouragement is a non-count noun. Notice the usage of *encouragement* in the sentences below:

Correct: Everyone needs encouragement.
Incorrect: Everyone needs the encouragement.
Incorrect: Everyone needs an encouragement.

Correct: Everyone needs encouragement from others.
Incorrect: Everyone needs the encouragement from others.

Of course, there are exceptions: "Everyone needs *the* encouragement of others" is only correct *with* the article.

📠 IT'S YOUR TURN

EXERCISE 3

Insert *a, an,* or *the* where appropriate in these sentences.

1. XYZ Corporation is 70 percent owned by public.

2. You need university education to become engineer.

3. Luz has Master of Business Administration (MBA) degree.

4. AGK is export-oriented company. Fertilizer is company's primary export.

5. Our team training records show that you still have not fulfilled 40-hour minimum requirement.

6. Early labor unions fought for eight-hour workday, but sometimes eight-hour day is simply not enough.

7. Regardless of amount, following extensions can be approved by Sun Bank.

8. Amount of down payment is substantial.

9. Leo refused to sign contract on advice of his lawyer.

📠 IT'S YOUR TURN

EXERCISE 4

The word *the* is used correctly in some places and incorrectly in others. Circle *the* where it is used correctly. Cross it out where it does not belong and add it where necessary.

1. With my long hours, I can hardly find the time for myself.

2. I can hardly find the time I need to complete this project.

3. Most recent upgrade was in the 2005.

4. Our products are all available through website.

5. I requested the guidance on this project.

6. Los Angeles has a growing problem with the pollution.

7. Smog is even denser now than it was five years ago.

8. Partnerships require the trust, communication, and contracts.

9. Imports come mainly from Europe, Japan, and the UK.

10. Although Maria gives the advice freely, she is often wrong.

PREPOSITIONS: SMALL WORDS, BIG CONNECTIONS

Prepositions are often confused. Understanding how and when these connecting words are used will add clarity to your writing. Prepositions are small, simple words that never change form.

about	behind	except	on	toward
above	below	for	onto	under
across	beneath	from	out	underneath
after	beside	in	outside	unlike
against	between	inside	over	until
along	beyond	into	past	up
among	by	like	regarding	upon
around	concerning	near	since	with
as	despite	next	through	within
at	down	of	throughout	without
before	during	off	to	

Examples of common prepositions and their uses.

Liu lives *in* New York. She comes *from* Taiwan.
The board meeting will be *at* 5:30.
The meeting is scheduled *for* 5:30.
Please put the report *in* the file.
Please leave the file *on* my desk.
I keep my cell phone *on* my desk when I'm at work.
My cell phone falls *off* my overcrowded desk.
I put my cell phone *in* my pocket when I leave.
I dropped my cell phone *into* a puddle this morning.
I got a new cell phone *from* a discount center online.
I see many similarities *among* the candidates.
I see many similarities *between* the candidates.
(*among* three or more; *between* two)

Understanding prepositions will help you as you continue to hone your skills. In the next chapter, you will be cutting prepositional phrases for conciseness.

The box is a good tool for visualizing and remembering prepositions of position:

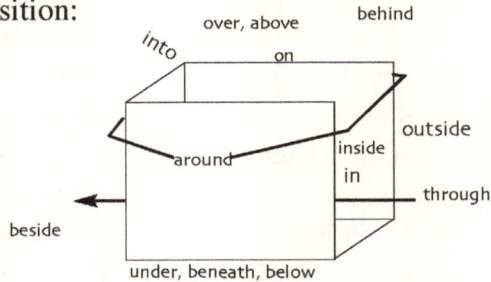

PREPOSITIONS ON THE GO*

By is often used before nouns when no article (*a, an, the*) is used. *On* and *in* are often used before articles, but note that *walking* is an exception.

If we are flying, we are going *by* plane.
on a plane.

If we are driving, we are going *by* car.
in a car.

If we are taking a bus, we are going *by* bus.
on a bus.

If we are taking a train, we are going *by* train.
on a train.

If we are walking, we are going *on* foot.

PREPOSITIONS OF PLACE

		Examples
in:	a country	*in* America
	a state	*in* New Jersey
	a county	*in* Union County
	a town	*in* Springfield
on:	a street	*on* Main Street
at:	an address	*at* 400 Main Street

**on the go*—moving quickly; traveling

PLACE OF WORK PREPOSITIONS

in:	a type of establishment	*in* an insurance company
	an industry	*in* insurance
on:	a task	*on* processing claims
at:	a specific establishment	*at* Ace Insurance Co.
		also *for* Ace Insurance
with	used with the verb to be	I am *with* Ace Insurance.
for	a specific establishment	I work *for* Ace Insurance.

PREPOSITIONS OF TIME

in:	a month	*in* April
	a season	*in* (the) spring
	a year	*in* 2008
	a century	*in* the 21st century
on:	a day	*on* Friday
	a date	*on* July 12, 2007
		on the first of the month
	a holiday	*on* Memorial Day
at	a time	*at* noon; at 12:00

IT'S YOUR TURN

EXERCISE 5

Correct these common preposition errors.

1. I'd like to introduce you with my cousin, Martha.

2. Workflow for one department to another is slow.

3. Please meet me next the cafeteria.

4. We have confidence on the new board member.

5. Production is scheduled to begin on January.

⌨ IT'S YOUR TURN

EXERCISE 6

Underline the correct prepositions.

1. Sales grew (at, to) $4M (in, on) July 2006.

2. Harry and I divided the workload (among, between) us.

3. The four of us share expenses equally (among, between) us.

4. Most of Marvin's data falls (upon, within) three categories.

5. I received a phone call (about, during) the budget.

6. I have been on this project team (since, from) last week.

7. The marketing report is (along, beside) the computer.

8. Our new brochure was created (by, from) Marie.

9. Ray's briefcase is (beneath, down) his desk.

10. The company cafeteria is (to, like) a four-star restaurant.

11. Jan put her umbrella (across, along) the aisle.

12. We want to familiarize you (of, with) our capabilities.

13. The report alerts all users (of, to) potential bugs.

14. Marcus fell asleep (from, during) the meeting.

IDIOMATIC USE OF PREPOSITIONS

Preposition use follows generally accepted idiomatic form. Listed on page 52 are some of the most often misused preposition combinations and their more acceptable replacements.

Remember, readers feel comfortable with correctly-formed sentences. The information in a sentence can become a secondary focus when the reader encounters unfamiliar usage and focuses on sentence structure instead of content.

COMMONLY CONFUSED PREPOSITIONS

Incorrect Use	Correct Use
according with	according to
acquaint to	acquaint with
angry at (a person)	angry with (a person)
authority about	authority on
build confidence of, to	build confidence in
conform in	conform to, with
deposit to (an account)	deposit in (an account)
different than	different from
in search for	in search of
in parallel with	parallel to
prior than	prior to
responsible on	responsible for
role on	role in
unequal for	unequal to

The use of different prepositions with the same key word may change the meaning of the word by limiting or clarifying it.

You agree
to a proposal
on a plan
with a person

We argue
for a principle
with a person

He differs
with [a person] (about or over a question)
from [something or someone]

She was impatient
for [something desired]
with [someone else]

He was rewarded
for something done
with a gift
by a person

Sales grew
to [an amount]
during [a time]

The company grew *in* stature; *in* influence, *in* popularity

We part
from [a person]
with [a thing]

⌨ IT'S YOUR TURN

EXERCISE 7

Fill in each blank with: *to, for, from, with, of,* or *since.*

1. Ira never agrees _____ John.

2. I will not agree _____ the conditions of this contract.

3. The Democratic governor will regularly differ _____ the Republican legislature.

4. Suzanne's idea of quality work differs _____ mine.

5. Ahmed is a free spirit. He has trouble conforming _____ the corporate structure.

6. According _____ this report, sales are up 34 percent.

7. Karthik will not part _____ his computer.

8. He would sooner part _____ his wife.

9. She is still in search _____ the perfect assistant.

10. Prior _____ the embezzlement charges, Bill was planning to retire in Hawaii.

11. I have complete confidence _____ your ability.

12. _____ 2006 our stock rose 7 percent _____ $15 per share.

13. Because of your outstanding achievement, we would like to present you _____ this award.

14. Our department manager is being recognized _____ her achievement _____ the CEO.

15. Your role _____ our success was invaluable.

PREPOSITION LOOSE ENDS *

Prepositions are often essential to sentence structure.
Incorrect: Most the company's designers work from home.
Correct: Most *of* the company's designers work from home.

The correct preposition can clarify and tighten your writing.
Incorrect: This new equipment will have a production
capacity to produce 54 million broilers.
Correct: This new equipment will have a production
capacity *of* 54 million broilers.
Or change your sentence structure:
Correct: This new equipment will have the capacity to
produce 54 million broilers.

**Prepositions often carry a greater burden* than they should,
resulting in awkward sentence structure.**
Incorrect: Management forged ahead and restructured with
disastrous results occurring.
Correct: Management forged ahead and restructured *with*
disastrous results.
Or change your sentence structure:
Correct: Management forged ahead and restructured;
disastrous results occurred.

Sometimes, prepositions are not needed at all.
Incorrect: We are comfortable *in* granting full support.
Incorrect: We are comfortable *for* granting full support.
Correct: We are comfortable (with) granting full support.

Incorrect: We are *near by* the factory.
Correct: We are *near* the factory.
Correct: The factory is nearby.

Incorrect: Despite of concerns, the merger was successful.
Correct: Despite concerns, the merger was successful.
Or change your sentence structure:
Correct: In spite of concerns, the merger was successful.

---

loose ends—unresolved or uncompleted details
carry a greater burden—to do more than a reasonable fair share

⊞ IT'S YOUR TURN

EXERCISE 8

Correct the preposition use in the following message. You may have to add, delete, or replace a preposition.

Subject: Capital Investments

With regard of our discussion about small capital investments, I recommend investment in Sunrise Enterprises. When this family-owned textile business went public at 14 months ago, it opened at $7^{1}/_{4}$ and now it has almost doubled to $13^{7}/_{8}$. According with its latest quarterly report, its debts are minimal. With regard of management and spending, its style is in alignment to our beliefs.

I will touch on base* with you next week concerning this and other investment opportunities. In that time, I will further acquaint you to Sun Enterprises and give you its fourth-quarter report.

EXERCISE 9

In this note, correct the preposition usage and missing articles and tighten by eliminating unnecessary prepositional phrases.

CREATIVE IMPORTS
patelscreativeimports.com

Dear Business Owner:

Thank you very much in visiting our booth at the New Jersey Procurement Fair at Taj Mahal Casino last month. We have taken on suggestions made by our customers and now offer more options and easy online orders to paypal.

If you have any questions, please call us in your convenience or e-mail info@patelscreativeimports.com.

We look forward to hearing from you.

Sincerely,
Pernita Patel
800-900-0000

---

touch base—to get in touch with; to communicate

PHRASAL VERBS

Phrasal verbs (two- and three-word verbs) are formed by adding
a preposition to the basic verb. Such two- and three-word verb
phrases are used like idioms; when the preposition and verb are
joined together, the verb phrase *takes on* a specific meaning different from that which the same words carry when separated.
For example, in the last sentence, takes on is a two-word verb
that means *acquire*. That meaning is slightly different from the
meaning of *to take (to grab, to seize, to get into one's hands)*.

A verb phrase may have more than one idiomatic meaning.
Take on, for example, also means to *assume as one's own;* that
meaning is often associated with *take on more responsibility*.

Like this example, two-word verbs are often transitive and are
used in sentences with direct objects.

       S   V   D.O.
The words *take on* meaning. (to acquire)

             S   V   D.O.
After Mira left, Jason *took on* her committee duties.
(to assume responsibility)

In these idiomatic, phrasal verbs, the preposition becomes part
of the verb. If it is followed by a noun, the noun is not the
object of a prepositional phrase; the noun is a direct object of
the phrasal verb.

The following sentences are examples of commonly used two-
word verb forms. If the verb takes a direct object in the sentence, the direct object is <u>underlined</u>. The verb's meaning is in
parentheses.

add up   The facts don't *add up*. (are not correct; don't make sense)

add in   The accountant *added in* (included) the 2006 <u>interest</u>.

allow for   Plans *allow for* (include provisions for; take into account) future <u>expansion</u>.

bring about Restructuring brings about (produces; induces) major
        <u>changes</u>.

In the next sentence, there is no direct object. The phrase following the two-word verb is a prepositional phrase introduced
by the preposition *with*; *call* is the object of the preposition
with. In the second "follow-up" sentence, *proposal* is a direct
object.

follow up   John will *follow up* (continue the effort) with a call.
        Raul *will follow up* (takes additional effort) the proposal
        with a call.

build up   After three years, interest *builds up* (increases).
        New evidence will *build up* (strengthen) the case.

IT'S YOUR TURN

EXERCISE 10

Write a sentence for each of the following two-word verbs.
Use a direct object in each sentence. The verb's meaning is
in parentheses.

1. call off (cancel)

2. carry out (complete, implement)

3. cash in (to receive profit, receive payment)

4. check out (investigate)

5. fill out (complete)

Sometimes a two-word verb is split by its direct object. If the direct object is in the form of a pronoun, the two-word verb **must** be split. Review the samples below. For good business writing style, use sentence #1 (direct object follows the entire verb) or use sentence #3 (direct object as a pronoun splitting the verb). More informal writing and conversational English often use sentence #2 versions. In writing, the #2 versions can present style problems, especially if the direct object phrase is a long one, as well as tone problems (too informal for some written communications).

look over (review)
1. Phil will *look over* the <u>contract</u>.
2. Phil will *look* the <u>contract</u> over.
3. Phil will *look* <u>it</u> over.
(*bad style:* Phil will *look* the latest version of the contract *over*.)

mark up (annotate *or* increase the price)
(annotate)
1. His editor *marked up* the <u>draft</u>.
2. His editor *marked* the <u>draft</u> up.
3. His editor *marked* <u>it</u> up.
(bad style: His editor *marked* the recently completed draft *up*.)
(increase the price)
1. The group *marked up* prescription <u>sleep aids</u> by 8 percent.
2. The group *marked* prescription <u>sleep aids</u> *up* by 8 percent.
3. The group *marked* <u>them</u> *up* by 20 percent.
(bad style: The group marked prescription <u>sleep aids</u> that just reached the market up by 8 percent.)

Try It

Write two sentences for each of the following two-word verbs, one with a direct object following the verb, one with the direct object as a pronoun that splits the verb.

cut out (eliminate)

_____

_____

point out (indicate)

_____

_____

take over (assume responsibility)

_____

_____

You may have written sentences like these:

cut out (eliminate)
These procedures *cut out* <u>waste</u>.
These procedures *cut* <u>it</u> *out*.

point out (indicate)
The consultants *pointed out* <u>weaknesses</u> in the system.
The consultants *pointed* <u>them</u> *out*.

take over (assume responsibility)
When Sonya left, Sebastian had to *take over* her duties.
The design department will *take* it *over*.

Not every two-word verb can be split by its direct object. As
with other idiomatic phrases, the specific meaning changes
when the words in the idiomatic verb phrase are separated. No
idiomatic three-word verbs can be split. Some examples of
such inseparable combinations are below. Write your own
example sentences for the last few.

agree on (agree)
The unions cannot *agree on* a <u>contract</u>.
They cannot *agree on* <u>it</u>.

pull through (survive a difficult situation)
By working weekends, the department *pulled through* the <u>crisis</u>
and delivered the product on time.

stand for (tolerate, represent)
(tolerate)   The client will not stand for any further delays.
(represent) The company logo stands for dependability.

Try It

break in on (interrupt)

_____

put up with (tolerate)

_____

give up on (abandon, cease work on)

_____

Following are a few more examples of verb phrases that are often used in business writing.

help out (assist)
Luiz's secretary will *help out* <u>Sam</u>. She will *help* <u>him</u> *out*.

hold out (stand firm)
His attorney insisted they *hold out* until the defendant agreed to a negotiated <u>settlement</u>.

keep down (reduce)
Acoustic tiles *keep down* <u>noise</u>. Tiles *keep* <u>it</u> *down*.

put together, pull together (create, organize, produce)
Simon's creative team *put together* a great <u>campaign</u>.
The team *put* <u>it</u> *together*.

write off (abandon, depreciate, concede to be lost)
We'll have to *write off* that <u>account</u> as a loss.
We'll have to *write* <u>it</u> *off*.

set up (make arrangements, assemble)
Can you help us *set up* the <u>conference</u>?
Please *set up* the <u>computer</u> for the presentation. Please *set* <u>it</u> *up*.

write up (report)
I'll *write up* the <u>meeting</u>.
Rose had to *write up* the disruptive <u>employee</u>.

Some phrasal verbs become so familiar that they enter the language as nouns, often hyphenated, and sometimes as a single word. Below are just a few popularly used verb-turned-nouns.

The project required careful *follow-up*.

Harrod's *markup* on that item was extremely high.

After such an extravagant *buildup* in the press, the actual conference was disappointing.

First Bank's *takeover* of Canterbury Trust surprised investors.

PRONOUNS: THE RIGHT SUBSTITUTES

Pronouns replace nouns. A pronoun takes its meaning from the noun for which it substitutes.

PRONOUNS HAVE SPECIFIC ROLES

Some pronouns act; some are acted upon; others show ownership. Each can do *only* its own job. Unlike the trend in today's business environment, pronouns cannot be cross-trained.* Those that act (subject pronouns) can *only* act; those that receive action (object pronouns) *only* receive action; those that show ownership (possessive pronouns) *only* show ownership.

---

*cross-trained—taught one another's jobs

Actors (Subjects)	Receivers (Objects)	Owners (Possessives)
I	me	my, mine
you (singular)	you (singular)	your, yours
he, she, it	him, her, it	his, her, hers, its
we	us	our, ours
you (plural)	you (plural)	your, yours
they	them	their, theirs
who	whom	whose

Most people use single pronouns correctly. Confusion occurs when a pronoun is accompanied by a proper noun.

For example:

John and (I, me) wrote the report.

Forget John for a moment and the choice is clear: *I* wrote the report. John cannot change that. With or without John, *I* wrote the report. *I* is a subject pronoun performing the action *wrote*.

What about object pronouns (receivers)?

Maria carpools with Joe and (I, me).

Let's forget Joe: Maria carpools with *me*. *Me* is an object pronoun (receiver). Me is the object of the preposition *with*. Whether or not Joe is in the car, Maria carpools with *me*.

Many speakers and writers of English as a second language confuse our gender pronouns.

	Male	Female	Neuter	Plural (All)
Subject	he	she	it	they
Object	him	her	it	them
Possessive	his	her (hers)	its	their (theirs)
		That is her office.		*That is their office.*
		That office is hers.		*That office is theirs.*

SELECTING THE CORRECT PRONOUN

He, him, and *his* are used to replace male nouns.
  Tom is retiring. *He* has been in this business for forty years.

She, her, and *hers* are used to replace female nouns.
  Tatita has no plans to retire. *She* loves her work.

It refers to things, not people.
  The Transit Company of North America added several bus lines. *It* [not *they*—meaning the Transit Company] met increased consumer demand.

Object pronouns do not follow verbs directly.

Incorrect: We suggested *them* to open an account.

In this sentence, we suggested *to them*, not suggested *them*.
Any of the sentences below can be used to convey this idea.

Correct: We suggested *to them* that opening an account was a good idea.

  We suggested *their* opening an account.

  We suggested *opening* an account.

  We suggested *that they* open an account.

Note: Pronouns that precede gerunds (verbs that end in *ing* and are used as nouns) are possessive pronouns; they modify a noun form (the gerund).

  I would appreciate *your* speaking at the conference.
  Our client requested *our* combining his two lines of credit.
  Sebastian rarely neglects *his* report writing.

The Mixed Gender Issue: English has no singular pronoun when the gender is unclear or could refer to either. Old-style writing would revert to masculine pronouns: *Each team member has **his** own unique style.* If all of the team members are men, this statement is fine. However, if the team consists of men *and* women or if you are *unsure*, use gender neutral statements instead of masculine. Using masculine statements to refer to "everyone" is now seen as old-style at best and, at worst, sexist; many people find it offensive.

Gender-neutral solutions include writing out *his or her*, writing *his/her*, or reframing (when possible) as a plural statement using *their* (which is gender neutral).

MYSELF MEANS ME, ALONE

Another category of pronouns is composed of pronouns that end in *-self*.

myself	ourselves
yourself	yourselves
himself	themselves
herself	
itself	
oneself	

Examples:

I went to the conference by *myself*.
(I went alone.)
Divide the project tasks among *yourselves*.
(Divide it among those of you working on it.)

You will see these pronouns incorrectly paired with nouns and with other pronouns.

Incorrect: Jim and myself will attend the conference.
Correct: Jim and *I* will attend the conference.

Incorrect: We divided the work between Jim and myself.
Correct: We divided the work between Jim and *me*.

PRONOUN CONSISTENCY

Be consistent in number. Singular nouns and pronouns must agree in number with the singular words to which they refer. Plurals must agree with plural words to which they refer.

Each officer must submit *his/her* report.
All officers must submit *their* reports.

Be careful of prepositional phrases that separate the pronoun from the word it refers to, even "understood" prepositional phrases, like those in the following sentences. A pronoun that follows a prepositional phrase must agree with the noun to which it refers, not the noun in the phrase.

One (of the officers) requested a report. *He* will receive it next week.

He agrees with the subject of the sentence (*one*), which is singular.

Several (of the officers) requested reports. *They* will receive them next week.

They agrees with the subject of the sentence (*several*), which is plural.

Be consistent in person. Pronouns and the nouns to which they refer must agree in "person."

When *I* arrive late, *I* have many messages waiting for *me*.

PRONOUNS THAT OWN (POSSESSIVES)

That book is *mine*; it is *my* book.
Your desk is *yours*.
Her cup is *hers*; *his* cup, however, is *his*.
Our car is *ours*, and *their* car is *theirs*.
Whose car is it, anyway?

These sentences illustrate the correct use of pronouns *that own*.

Joyce's office is not downtown. *Her* office is in the countryside. *Hers* is a charming office.

Tapas left *his* briefcase in the conference room. The briefcase you found must be *his*.

When your clients arrive, please give them *their* copies of the report. The copies on the conference table are *theirs*.

🖥 IT'S YOUR TURN

EXERCISE 11

Replace each underlined noun with the correct pronoun.

1. The promotion was offered to <u>Mira</u>.

2. The promotion was offered to Wayne and <u>Mira.</u>

3. The changes will benefit everyone in <u>Owen's</u> department.

4. The business planner suggested that <u>Maria</u> take a basic accounting course.

5. I called this meeting to discuss the prospective takeover and to answer any questions you have about <u>the takeover</u>.

🖥 IT'S YOUR TURN

EXERCISE 12

Complete each sentence with a correct pronoun.

1. Hiroko is a stronger manager than _____ .

2. The project coordinator divided the responsibilities between José and _____ .

3. Every employee must use _____ time effectively.

4. The sister company in India has increased _____ sales 21 percent.

5. AZ Corp's annual report indicated that _____ profits were up.

6. After QT Co. failed in 2003, several of _____ former top executives established a new, successful enterprise.

7. All employees must wear _____ security badges.

8. The secretary made reservations for Shu and _____.

EXERCISE 1

1. general
2. specific
3. specific

EXERCISE 2

1. Corporations are the new leaders in legislation.
2. The corporations in this organization are socially responsible.

EXERCISE 3

1. XYZ Corporation is 70% owned by *the* public.

2. You need *a* university education to become *an* engineer.

3. Luz has *a* Master of Business Administration (MBA) degree. *or* Luz has *an* MBA degree.

4. AGK is *an* export-oriented company. Fertilizer is *the* company's primary export.

5. Our team training records show that you still have not fulfilled *the* 40-hour minimum requirement.

6. Early labor unions fought for *an (the)* eight-hour work day, but sometimes *an (the)* eight-hour day is simply not enough.

7. Regardless of *the* amount, *the* following extensions can be approved by Sun Bank.

8. *The* amount of *the* down payment is substantial.
   or *The* down payment is substantial.

9. Leo refused to sign *the* contract on *the* advice of his lawyer. ("on advice" is often used without an article—*the*—in the phrase "on advice of his lawyer.")

EXERCISE 4

(Articles that were used correctly are shown here in italics.)

1. With my long hours, I can hardly find ~~the~~ time for myself.
2. I can hardly find *the* time I need to complete this project.

3. *The* most recent upgrade was in ~~the~~ 2005.
4. Our products are all available through *the* website.
5. I requested ~~the~~ guidance on this project.
6. Los Angeles has a growing problem with ~~the~~ pollution.
7. *The* smog is even denser now than it was five years ago.
8. Partnerships require ~~the~~ trust, communication, and contracts.
9. Imports come mainly from Europe, Japan, and the UK.
10. Although Maria gives ~~the~~ advice freely, she is often wrong.

EXERCISE 5

1. I'd like to introduce you *to* my cousin, Martha.
2. Workflow *from* one department to another is slow.
3. Please meet me next *to* the cafeteria.
4. We have confidence *in* the new board members.
5. Production is scheduled *to* begin *in* January.

EXERCISE 6

1. to, in
2. between
3. among
4. within
5. about
6. since
7. beside
8. by
9. beneath
10. like
11. across
12. with
13. to
14. during

EXERCISE 7

1. with
2. to
3. with
4. from
5. to
6. to
7. with (part *with* a thing)
8. from (part *from* a person)
9. of
10. to
11. in
12. since, to
13. with
14. for, by
15. in

EXERCISE 8

With regard *to* our discussion about small capital investments, I recommend that you invest in Sunrise Enterprises. When this family-owned textile business went public ~~at~~ 14 months ago, it opened at $7^{1}/_{4}$ and now has almost doubled to $13^{7}/_{8}$. According *to* its latest quarterly report, its debts are minimal. With regard *to* management and spending, its style is in alignment *with* our beliefs.

I will touch base with you next week concerning this and other investment opportunities. At that time, I will further acquaint you *with* Sun Enterprises and give you its fourth-quarter report.

EXERCISE 9

Dear Business Owner:

Thank you very much *for* visiting our booth at the New Jersey Procurement Fair at the Taj Mahal Casino last month.

We have taken ~~on~~ customer suggestions and now offer more options and easy online ordering *through* paypal. If you have any questions, please call us at your convenience or e-mail info@patelscreativeimports.com.

We look forward to hearing from you.

Sincerely,
Pernita Patel
800-900-0000

EXERCISE 10

1. We called off the auditions.
2. The new director will carry out the terms of the agreement.
3. It's time to cash in your chips.
4. The employee relations committee checks out all reports of discrimination.
5. Applicants fill out three forms. Adding a computer technician fills out the team.

EXERCISE 11

1. her
2. her
3. his
4. she
5. it

EXERCISE 12

1. he (I, she)
2. me (him, her)
3. his or her (his/her)
   or use plural (All... their)
4. its
5. its
6. its
7. their
8. me (him, her, them, us)

Structure: The Right Place at the Right Time

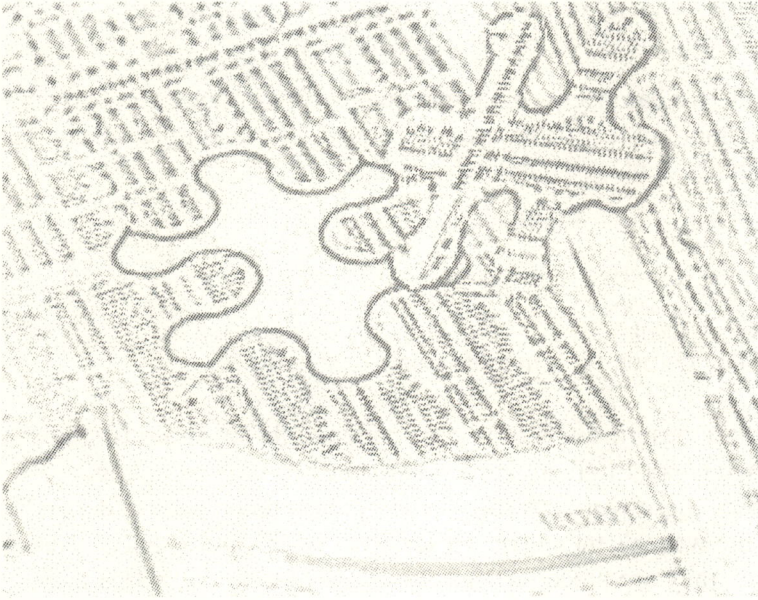

SENTENCE PATTERNS

Direct translations mirror first language sentence patterns, which differ from English sentence patterns. Following is a direct translation (to English from an Asian language) of a simple sentence using descriptive words.

> Company of the family manufactures primarily machines for tool and dye making.

While we can decipher the meaning, word order, style, and grammar are lost if the translator does not account for American language sentence patterns.

Here is a simple English sentence pattern.

SUBJECT	VERB	OBJECT
who or what	does	what
(actor)	(action)	(receives action)
The company	manufactures	machines.

Adding descriptive words can challenge those whose first language is not English. Placement is key to understanding. Where these words fit into the simple sentence pattern depends on the writer's meaning. Descriptive words are usually clearest when they are placed as closely as possible to the words they describe.

ADJECTIVE	ADVERB	ADJECTIVE
(describes)	(describes)	(describes)
family-owned	primarily	tool and dye

The ^ company ^ manufactures ^ machines.

Following the sentence pattern shown above, the original direct translation has been corrected and clarified. Note the changes:

Company of the family → *The family-owned company*
manufacturers primarily → *primarily manufactures*
machines for tool and dye making → *tool and dye machines*

WORDS THAT DESCRIBE—ADJECTIVES & ADVERBS

Specific kinds of descriptors are not only placed close to the words they modify, they also have a usual position either before or after that word.

Adjectives usually precede nouns.

> The owner pays $900 in *related* expenses.
> BBR has invested *approximately* $4 million.

Adverbs sometimes precede and sometimes follow verbs.

> Import trade is *greatly* affected by duties.
> Import trade is affected *greatly* by duties.
> Imports will *rapidly* decline.
> Imports will decline *rapidly*.

If adjectives and adverbs are not as close as possible to the words they describe, the meaning of the sentence is harder to determine. Look at this sentence:

H Corp. has been operating in Ohio since 1995 profitably.

The reader has to search for the word described by *profitably*. *Profitably* describes *operating*:

H Corp. has been *operating profitably* in Ohio since 1995.

PHRASES THAT DESCRIBE

Prepositional phrases also describe nouns (see Chapter 3 for *prepositions* defined). Here are some examples.

The results *of the study* were conclusive.

Many *of the stockholders* attended the annual meeting.

DOUBLE PATTERNS

I know *how* should be done the report.

s v   s   v
I know [how] <u>the report should be done</u>.

Try it:

That is [how] began the data collection process.

      s   v   s   v

_____ _____ [   ]_____ _____

s v   s   v
That is [how] the data collection process began.

CUTTING WORDINESS

PREPOSITIONAL PHRASES

As you saw in the Chapter 3, prepositions are essential connecting words. Prepositional *phrases* are useful, but often unnecessarily wordy. In concise writing, one challenge is to cut unnecessary prepositional phrases. They are like speed bumps, slowing the reader down. Of course, you don't want to cut all, but you do want to limit the number you use. Study the examples:

Selling *in the global market* requires awareness *of diversity among cultures.*

Selling *globally* requires *cultural diversity awareness.*

Usually, you can change a prepositional phrase into a single- or double-word modifier.

the manager *of the bank* ➤ the *bank* manager
the class *in accounting* ➤ the *accounting* class
the production *of cotton* ➤ *cotton* production
the plan *for the building* ➤ the *office complex* building plan
of an office complex

Try it:

Import trade *in Europe* is greatly affected by an increase *in import duties*.

_____

_____

You can tighten the above sentence by changing the prepositional phrases to single- and double-word modifiers.

European import trade is greatly affected by an *import-duty* increase.

What changed?

1. The prepositional phrases in the original sentence followed the nouns they described. The single- (or double-) word modifiers in the rewrite precede the nouns they describe.

2. Note subtle changes in individual words:

   Import trade i*n Europe* ⟶ *European* import trade
   an increase in *import duties* ⟶ an *import-duty* increase

   Duties is a plural noun in the phrase on the left. *Import-duty* is an adjective describing *increase*; adjectives don't have singular and plural forms in English.

3. In some cases, when two words combine to form an adjective, those words are hyphenated.

   increase in import duties ⟶ *import-duty increase*

Prepositional phrases are not incorrect, but too many in one sentence make the sentence harder to read. In addition, preposition use is often idiomatic: it follows general usage patterns. For example, we say "a two-story building" rather than "a building of two stories."

IT'S YOUR TURN

EXERCISE I

Tighten the following sentences by eliminating the awkward prepositional phrases in favor of single- or double-word modifiers.

1. The supervisor of the work team called a meeting.

2. Increased profits in 2006 resulted from the company's expansion of its domestic market and the building of new factories in the domestic locations.

3. Sun exports on a regular basis.

4. Manna produces fabric for dresses.

5. The current market displays high volatility in price.

6. Kato Corporation's main business is the production of shrimp feed.

7. The market dropped 2,000 points in index.

8. The complex has 600 units of apartments.

9. In Hong Kong, we stayed at a hotel of four stars.

10. Reddy Corporation will only sign a lease of 30 years.

11. Joe built 12 stories of office building.

MORE MODIFIERS—FORMING COMPOUND WORDS

Notice that in forming compound words, the modifier is placed before the word it describes. The main focus of a compound is the second half. The first half usually answers the question "What kind?" Look at these examples from page 74:

manager What kind of manager? a *bank* manager
class What kind of class? an *accounting methods* class

If the sequence is changed, sense is lost, or, in some cases, meaning changes.

> fire house (a station for firefighters & equipment)
> ≠ house fire (a fire in a house)

> office complex (a group of office buildings)
> ≠ complex office (a complicated office)

Example

First, highlight or circle all prepositions in the paragraph below. Then streamline* the sentences by changing the prepositional phrases into nouns with a single- or double-word modifier. Then, check your answer against the corrected example.

The technical assistant of the engineering department has developed a manual of procedures for employees in the temporary pool. The department of engineering designs specifications for buildings and renovations.

Corrected Example:

The engineering department's technical assistant developed a procedure manual for temporary pool employees. The engineering department designs building and renovation specifications.

What changed?

1. *technical assistant of the engineering department* → engineering department's technical assistant

2. *manual of procedures* → procedure manual

3. *employees in the temporary pool* → temporary pool employees

4. *department of engineering* → engineering department

5. *specifications for building and renovations* → building and renovation specifications

---

streamline—to get rid of excess

FORMING QUESTIONS

We talked about the simple sentence pattern of subject, verb, object. That pattern sometimes shifts when statements are turned into questions.

CLOSED QUESTIONS WITH *To Be*

Closed questions elicit short yes/no answers. In a statement, the verb comes after the subject. Questions are not as consistent. When *to be* is the verb in a question, that verb comes before the subject, reversing the usual subject-verb pattern.

Statement: Nina is a strong manager.

Question: Is Nina a strong manager?

Statement: Our company picnic is today.

Question: Is our company picnic today?

To be does not, however, always stand alone. It is often used as what is called a "helping verb." When *to be* or another helping verb is used, think of the verb as having two parts. The first part of the verb (*to be*) comes before the subject in question word order. The second part remains after the subject, in its original position.

Statement: Nina is going to be a strong manager.

Question: Is Nina going to be a strong manager?

Statement: Our company picnic is cancelled today.

Question: Is our company picnic cancelled today?

Statement: The team-building seminar will be held at The Hilton.

Question: Will the team-building seminar be held at The Hilton?

OPEN QUESTIONS

Open questions elicit answers of more than a few words. Often, they begin with the words *what*, *why*, or *how*. *How do you plan to raise the money?* is an open question. Open questions not only elicit a more in-depth response than closed, they also leave open more possibilities for different responses. A closed question may, as in the case below, suggest an answer rather than allowing for a more thoughtful response.

Most questions use the verb-subject sentence pattern.

S   V

Statement: This year, our conference theme is peace.

              V   S

Closed question: Did you choose the theme because of current events?
Possible answers: *Yes. / No.*

             V   S

Open question: Why did you choose peace as a theme?
Possible answer (one of many): *We have been wanting to use this theme for a number of years because... Of course, recent events influenced our choice, however...*

To be questions that begin with *who, what, when, where, or how* use the verb-subject sentence pattern.

           S   V

Statement: Maria was in Amsterdam.

                 V   S

Question: How long was Maria in Amsterdam?

                 S   V

Incorrect: How long Maria was in Amsterdam?

Future tense questions divide the verb into two parts and use the structure VSV:

                    S   V

Statement: The team building seminar will be inspirational.

           V1   S   V2

Question 1: Will the team building seminar be inspirational?

           V1   S   V2

Question 2: How will the team building seminar be inspirational?

🖳 IT'S YOUR TURN

EXERCISE 2

Rewrite the statements as questions. Write one closed and one open question for each statement.

1. The President is going to lower the deficit.

2. Vi is a good candidate for promotion.

3. The policies need to be revised.

4. The company plans to improve its customer service.

5. CCT is creating a new marketing strategy.

6. Marie is writing an article for the newsletter.

Do: A TENSE JOB

These questions can be open or closed. For example:

> *Did you* promote Paul? (closed)
> *Why did you* promote Paul? (open)

To do questions are tricky because the main verb has no tense. The word *do* actually has the responsibility of showing the tense of the verb in the sentence.

Example:

Present:
Statement: John delegates report writing.
Question: *Does* John *delegate* report writing?

Past:
Statement: John delegated report writing.
Question: Did John delegate report writing?

Notice that in the first statement, the verb is in the present tense, *delegates*. When changed into a question with do, *delegate* is without tense and *do* becomes present tense, *does*. In the second, *delegated* is past tense; in the question, *did* takes on the past and *delegate* is without tense. (This is called the base form of the verb form and is discussed in Chapter 5.)

Here are the steps to changing a statement to a closed *to do* question.

Statement: He left at six.

> Step 1. Add *do* (*do, does,* or *did*) before the subject.
> *Did* he (left) at six?

> Step 2. Change the verb.
> *leave*
> Did he ~~left~~ leave at six?

AVOID CONFUSION

Statement:	You *came* in early this morning.
Closed question:	*Did* you *come* in early this morning?
Open question:	When *did* you *come* in this morning?
Incorrect:	When you came in?
	When did you came in?

Statement:	I *arrived* in the United States in 1996.
Closed question:	*Did* you *arrive* in the United States in 1996?
Open question:	When *did* you *arrive* in the United States?
Incorrect:	When you arrived in the United States?

🖳 IT'S YOUR TURN

EXERCISE 3

Part 1: Turn the following statements into two questions: one open and one closed. Remember, word order and verb form may change. The first one is done for you.

1. Toti studied graphic design.
   Closed: Did Toti study graphic design?
   Open: What did Toti study?

2. He manages his time effectively.

3. After surveying the property, Toglia Inc. decided not to buy.

4. Allan does not think we can afford another computer.

5. Our office holiday party includes dinner.

6. Marion writes our company's "tech notes" blog.

7. Emilia prefers the last software version.

Part 2: Correct the following questions. Sometimes you will have to change the verb form, sometimes the sentence pattern.

1. How long you stayed in India last summer?

2. When did you completed the report?

3. Where you are from?

4. Who does supervise you?

5. What from the error problems resulted?

6. You do think the idea it is good?

7. When the restaurant will close?

8. Why you do want those figures?

9. Whom we can ask for advice?

10. Why the meeting is so long?

IT'S JUST THE WAY WE SAY IT! THE AMERICAN IDIOM

IDIOMS

If learning the meaning of each word in a phrase does not help you unlock its meaning, chances are you have encountered an idiom. Sometimes, the reason for using a particular phrase is simply, "That's the way we say it."

Idioms result from frequent usage. Some defy logical explanation; others just aren't worth the time to analyze. Accept them and learn them.

Books on idioms abound and you have seen more footnoted throughout this book. All footnotes are in the "Glossary of Idioms," along with definitions of the idioms below.

Sports idioms common in American business language:

out in left field	shotgun approach
off base	on the ball
three strikes	the ball is in your court
all your ducks in a row	on target
saved by the bell	step up to the plate
slam dunk	in the ball park

Some other common idioms:

go through channels	dig in your heels
back burner	can't put two and two together
burn out	too much on your plate
burn up	chain of command
miss the boat	slow burn

🖥 IT'S YOUR TURN

EXERCISE 4

Correct the following idiom errors.* The first two are corrected for you.

1. Mr. Yu started his business from a scratch.
   Mr. Yu started his business from scratch.

2. Although this project is difficult, let's remain stick.
   Although this project is difficult, let's stick with it.

3. You stuck your neck up for me. Thanks.

4. As the matter of fact, I was born in Tokyo.

5. When the marketing and finance departments joined in their forces, they developed a creative plan.

6. We can solve the dispute with an approach of three prongs.

7. Last year our numbers were in red.

8. We expect to break even this quarter, but projected sales could put us in black within a few months.

9. Sales usually fall out this time of year, but this year we hope to buck up the trend with our new software release.

---

* For definitions of these and other idioms in this chapter, see the *Glossary of Idioms*.

PUTTING RESPONSIBILITY INTO THE BUSINESS DOCUMENT

ACTIVE VOICE

The passive voice is sorely* overused and misused in American business writing. Even the forthright American writer shies away from* the active voice—the voice of responsibility.

In active voice, the "star" (the actor) is up front, in front of the verb/action of the sentence. Passive voice shoves the actor out of the front position to the end of the sentence. Often, the "star," the one doing the action, is left out entirely.

Example: Every time the program is used, errors occur.

After reading the above sentence, the reader still does not know *who* is using this program. A question remains in the reader's mind because the sentence is in passive voice: *the program* is not performing the action, *use.* The actor (the one *using*) is unknown, *not included in the sentence at all.*

How could you correct that sentence? One solution is to keep the sentence passive but to add the actor (the one using the program) to the end: *Errors occur every time the program is used by José.* A clearer correction puts the actor up front: *Every time José uses the program, errors occur.*

Writers aren't always trying to duck* responsibility. Passive voice sentences become a writing habit because business readers are used to reading such sentences. They clutter all sorts of business documents.

---

sorely—to a great extent
shy away from—to avoid
duck—to avoid

Examples:

1. **Contracts:** All payments by the purchaser will be applied to the current account within five days of receipt of payment. (Applied by whom?)

2. **Policy Guidelines:** Reports of sexual harassment are to be investigated promptly. (Investigated by whom?)

3. **Analysis Reports**: A slight rise in temperature was recorded ten minutes after inoculation. *(Recorded by whom?)*

Each of the above sentences, as official as it sounds, omits a critical piece of information: by whom? As in many passive sentences, the one doing the action is missing from the sentence. Someone is responsible for applying the payment, for investigating the sexual harassment report, for recording the elevated temperature, but the sentences don't tell who.

Example:

Discounts were offered to clear out old stock. *Who offered?*

Central Software offered discounts to clear out old stock.

🖥 IT'S YOUR TURN

EXERCISE 5

Rewrite sentences 1-3 in active voice. Put the star up front so he or she can take responsibility for the action.

1. All purchase payments will be applied to the current account within five days of receipt of payment by the accounting department.

2. Reports of sexual harassment will be investigated promptly by the personnel manager.

3. A number of bugs in the new anti-virus software are being found by users.

WHEN PASSIVE IS THE VOICE OF CHOICE

Passive voice is not always inappropriate. If knowing who or what is performing the action is unimportant to the reader and you wish to emphasize the object (the receiver), passive voice may strengthen the passage. The example below illustrates a sentence where passive voice is more to the point.

The ticket was issued on June 9, 2006.   [passive]
The officer issued the ticket on June 9, 2006. [active]

In sentence 3 of the examples at the top of page 86, passive voice is also a better choice than the active voice rewrite *if* the reader doesn't need to know who recorded the temperature. The important information, what was recorded, remains in the star position. If the scientist were sure about the cause, or brave enough, he or she could report the information in this interesting, active voice version: *The inoculation caused a slight temperature rise within ten minutes.*

IT'S YOUR TURN

EXERCISE 6

Turn the passive sentences into active sentences. You will have to select the actor for each sentence.

1. A joint venture with Fuji Bank Ltd. was entered into.

2. The recommendations were proposed last Friday.

3. Rail connections were suspended.

Although passive voice has its place, a good active voice sentence tells the reader more than a passive one. Be careful not to become a habitual user of passive voice sentences.

🖳 IT'S YOUR TURN

EXERCISE 7

In the following e-mail, passive voice sentences are marked by a
(P). Change at least half of them to active voice. Decide which
ones to change based on which you believe will be more useful to
the reader *or* which improves the writing style.

Subject: Spanish Information Packets

Dear Sean,

(P) Our Spanish advertising pilot program for the Jersey City
Hospital will be launched by the BC Agency on June 2 with
full-page ads in El Nuevo Hudson and Noticias del Mondo.
(P) The new primary care clinic will be featured in the ads, as
will the availability of Spanish-speaking doctors. (P) A new
800 number was arranged for and will be answered by Spanish
operators.

(P) One thousand Spanish information packages should be
delivered to the hospital's mail center, Attn: Corporate
Services. (P) The remainder of the print order (9,000 information packages) should be delivered to the warehouse at 445
North Bond Street, Newark, NJ 07503, Attn: M. Cohen.

(P) Before any of the print order is released for delivery, five
samples should be sent to our agency for review by me.

Please call if you have any questions.

Regards,

Diana

PARALLEL STRUCTURE: KEEPING YOUR LANGUAGE IN LINE *

By describing like ideas in similar terms, the writer helps the reader. Just as we try to keep pronouns in agreement with each other and our subjects in agreement with verbs, writers try to keep statements parallel:

Parallel: Luz types well, organizes efficiently, and answers the phone professionally.

Not parallel: Luz is a good typist, organizes efficiently, and answers the telephone in a professional manner.

IT'S YOUR TURN

EXERCISE 8

Edit the following paragraph, creating parallel structure.

Sam, our new clerical assistant, answers the phones and has responsibility for photocopying documents. Sam attends a local university three evenings a week, is available to us four afternoons a week, and his father has his help on weekends.

PARALLEL LISTS

Parallel structure is particularly effective for bulleted lists. If items in a list are in parallel form, each sounds equally important, and the list is easier to scan. Read the following list aloud and then read the parallel version aloud. Can you hear the difference?

---

keep in line—to keep in its place, or keep as it should be

Not Parallel: The committee's discussion focused on benefits of the new program:
- allowing multiple user access
- to reduce input time
- capabilities that provide upgraded test results

Parallel: The committee's discussion focused on benefits of the new program:
- *multiple user* access
- *reduced input* time
- *upgraded test* results

The specific parallel structure form you choose is not important. Several different parallel forms can be equally effective for the list above.

Also Parallel: The committee's discussion focused on benefits of the new program:
- *allowing* multiple user access
- *reducing* input time
- *upgrading* test results

Also Parallel: The committee's discussion focused on benefits of the new program:
- *to allow* multiple user access
- *to reduce* input time
- *to upgrade* test results

If the writer had decided to give the information in paragraph form instead of as a bulleted list, the information would still be easier to follow in its new parallel form. Compare these two versions. The second, parallel sentence is a smoother read.

The committee's discussion focused on the benefits of the new program, which are multiple user access, reducing input time, and capabilities that upgrade test results.

The committee's discussion focused on the benefits of the new program, which are multiple user access, reduced input time, and upgraded test results.

IT'S YOUR TURN

EXERCISE 9

In this e-mail, the supervisor's directions to his assistant would be clearer and stronger in parallel structure. Edit for clarity and conciseness and pay special attention to rewriting the starred* sentences using parallel structure. **Hint:** When rewriting in parallel structure forms, you should expect to cut extra words from the sentences.

Subject: W.R. James Proposal

Dear Monique,

Our department must make a recommendation concerning this proposal by Monday. Please bring together those to whom we sent the draft for review and call a meeting to work out final issues before I write our recommendation. *Before the meeting, I want you to prepare an agenda, also you are reviewing the proposal, and any outstanding questions that it raises should be listed.

*When you invite them to the meeting, please notify the appropriate people that we still need a definite legal opinion, to assemble the financial statement that is most current, and complete patent documentation. With all this information at the meeting, we should be able to develop a final recommendation.

Regards,

Anita

🖳 IT'S YOUR TURN

EXERCISE 10

Rewrite each paragraph in the message below using parallel structure in either sentence form or in bulleted list form.

RECOMMENDATION TO MOVE INTO SMALLER OFFICE SPACE

Before we sign the new lease, I suggest we consider looking for smaller office space. We have been underutilizing the space we have for the past few years. We no longer invite clients in as most of our business is conducted through the internet. Several key employees are now working from home and the meeting room is never used anymore.

With the money we could save on rent, we can upgrade our online presence, increase funds for our marketing campaigns, and be ready for bringing the business to another level.

EXERCISE 1

1. The work team supervisor called a meeting.
2. Increased profits resulted from the company's domestic market expansion and building new domestic factories.
3. Sun exports regularly.
4. Manna produces dress fabric.
5. The current market displays high price volatility.
6. Kato Corporation's main business is shrimp feed production.
7. The market dropped 2,000 index points.
8. The complex has 600 apartment units.
9. In Hong Kong, we stayed at a four-star hotel.
10. Reddy Corporation will only sign a 30-year lease.
11. Joe built a 12-story office building.

EXERCISE 2

1. Closed: Is the president going to lower the deficit?
   Open: How is the president going to lower the deficit?
2. Closed: Is Vi a good candidate for promotion?
   Open: Why is Vi a good candidate for promotion?
3. Closed: Do the policies need to be revised?
   Open: Why do the policies need to be revised?
4. Closed: Does the company plan to improve its customer service?
   Open: How does the company plan to improve its customer service?
5. Closed: Will CCT's new marketing strategy include monthly emails offering specials and highlighting new items?
   Open: What will CCT's new marketing strategy involve?
6. Closed: Is Marie writing an article for the newsletter?
   Open: What is Marie writing? *or* What kind of article is Marie writing?

ANSWER KEY

EXERCISE 3

Part 1

Suggested answers; your questions may vary.

2. Closed: Does he manage his time effectively?

   Open: How does he manage his time?

3. Closed: After surveying the property, did Toglia Inc. decide not to buy? *or* Did Toglia Inc. decide not to buy after surveying the property?

   Open: Why did Toglia Inc. decide not to buy after surveying the property?

4. Closed: Doesn't Allan think we can afford another computer?

   Open: Why doesn't Allan think we can afford another computer?

5. Closed: Does our office holiday party include dinner?

   Open: What does our office party include?

6. Closed: Does Marion write our company's "Tech Notes" blog?

   Open: Who writes our company's "Tech Notes" blog?

7. Closed: Does Emilia prefer the last software version?

   Open: Why does Emilia prefer the last software version?

Part 2

1. How long did you stay in India last summer?
2. When did you complete the report?
3. Where are you from?
4. Who supervises you?
5. What problems resulted from the error?
6. Do you think the idea is good?
   or Do you think it is a good idea?
7. When will the restaurant close?
8. Why do you want those figures?
9. Whom can we ask for advice?
10. Why is the meeting so long?

EXERCISE 4

3. You stuck your neck *out* for me. Thanks.
4. As *a* matter of fact, I was born in Tokyo.
5. When the marketing and finance departments *joined forces*, they developed a creative plan.
6. We can solve the dispute with a *three-pronged approach.*
7. Last year, we were *in the red.*
8. We expect to break even this quarter, but projected sales could put us *in the black* within a few months.
9. Sales usually *fall off* this time of year, but this year we hope to *buck the trend* with our new software release.

EXERCISE 5

1. The accounting department will apply all purchase payments to the current account within five days of receipt of payment.
2. The personnel manager will promptly investigate reports of sexual harassment.
3. Users are finding a number of bugs in the new anti-virus software.

EXERCISE 6

Suggested answers. You came up with different names.

1. We entered into a joint venture with Fiji Bank Ltd.
2. Charles proposed the recommendations last Friday.
3. Macro Transit suspended rail connections.

EXERCISE 7

Subject: Spanish Information Packets

Dear Sean,

The BC Agency will launch our company's Spanish advertising pilot program for the Jersey City Hospital on June 2 with full-page ads in El Nuevo Hudson and Noticias del Mondo. Ads will feature the new primary care clinic and the availability of Spanish-speaking doctors. The agency arranged for a new 800 number that will be answered by Spanish operators.

Please send (or have the printer send) 1000 Spanish information packages to he hospital's mail center, Attn: Corporate Services.

Deliver the remainder of the print order (9,000 collated information packages) to the warehouse at 445 North Bond Street,
Newark, NJ 07503, Attn: M. Cohen.

Before releasing any of the print order for delivery, send five
samples to our agency for my review. (or—"Before you release
any of the print order, send five samples to me at our agency
for review.")

Please call if you have any questions.

Regards,

Diana

EXERCISE 8

Sam, our new clerical assistant, answers the phones and photo-
copies documents. Sam attends a local university three
evenings a week, works for us four afternoons a week, and
helps his father on weekends.

EXERCISE 9

Subject: W.R. James Proposal

Dear Monique,

Our department must make a recommendation concerning this
proposal by Monday. Please *invite* everyone to whom we sent
the *review draft* to a meeting to work out final issues before I
write our recommendation. Before the meeting please prepare
an agenda, review the proposal, and list any outstanding questions.

When you invite them to the meeting, please notify the appropriate people that we still need a definite legal opinion, the current financial statement, and complete patent documentation.
[The parallel pattern in this rewrite is two modifiers plus noun:
definite legal opinion, etc.] Having all this information at the
meeting will help us develop a final recommendation.

Regards,

Anita

EXERCISE 10

RECOMMENDATION TO MOVE INTO
SMALLER OFFICE SPACE

Before we sign the new lease, I suggest we consider smaller office space. We have been underutilizing the space we have for the past few years.

- We no longer invite clients in (most of our business is conducted through the internet).
- Several key employees now work from home.
- No one uses the meeting room any more.

With the money we save on rent, we can upgrade our online presence, increase funds for our marketing campaigns, and bring the business to another level.

Verbs & Simple Tenses

PRECISE TENSE = CLARITY

English verbs convey a great deal of information about exactly *when* things happen. They do this through precise changes in tense in verb form. These verb forms can be difficult to learn. Tense, however, works as a valuable source of information for the reader *because* the verb form is so exact in its precise time reference. To misuse the verb form, the tense, is to mislead the reader about when something is happening, has happened, or will happen.

To simplify the complicated verb use in English, many teachers emphasize that consistency is the guide: "Be consistent in time; if you begin in the past tense, continue in the same tense." That rule is valid only as long as you are describing things that actually happened at the *same time*.

> I *attended* the meeting yesterday, and Mr. Finch *said* to extend the deadline. Several managers *spoke* at the meeting, and they *related* the problems to safety hazards.

Because all the actions described in this paragraph took place at yesterday's meeting, all are reported in the same tense—*past tense*.

Determining the correct tense is not always that simple. Quite often, several different times are expressed in the same paragraph, and the verb form must shift to refer accurately to *actual time*.

You will see several examples in the Chapter 6 section: Shifting Tenses, on page 125.

In all languages, *tense equals time*. English uses direct time references as a starting point and then uses the verb form to do much more. Mastering the different tenses will add clarity to your writing.

PAST   PAST
I *attended* the meeting yesterday, and Joe Grimes *spoke* about
                    FUTURE   PAST
the merger that *will take place* in October. He *said* that it
PRESENT
is now the most important item on our agenda, and that your

                  PRESENT
department *is* responsible for contract preparation.

            FUTURE
You *will present* drafts to Mr. Grimes for approval, and he
PAST   PRESENT
stressed that he *wants* them on his desk by next Friday.

When writers use the correct verb form, they add clarity and
precision to their sentences, conveying the very important dis-
tinctions of time that English verb tenses are designed to convey. To achieve such precision, each verb form must be used
correctly to reflect its own, specific time as the verbs do in the
sample paragraph about Joe Grimes.

For an ESL writer, accurately reporting time through correct
tense is just the beginning of verb mastery because tense is not
always simply a report of actual time. For instance, perfect
tenses show the relationship of one time in the sentence to
another. Tense can also indicate the *status* of a reported situation or indicate factual information. Adding specific auxiliary
words to verbs further alters meaning.

Each tense presents trouble spots for many ESL writers. Rather
than attempting to discuss every aspect of correct tense usage,
this chapter isolates a few of the most troublesome "tense"
issues for ESL writers.

TENSE BASICS

To begin at the beginning, the simplest form of a verb is the base form. When the base form is preceded by "to," it is called the infinitive.

plan [base form]   to plan [infinitive]

Base forms and infinitives have many special uses in English; we will discuss them in connection with the verb tense in which they cause the most confusion.

THE TIME IS NOW—
PRESENT TENSE

Regular present tense verbs use a consistent form *except* in the third person singular. In third person singular, the verb changes by adding a final *s*. Confusion about noun/verb agreement arises because most noun plurals also end in *s*. In English, verbs are the opposite. Verbs in the present tense third person *singular* end in *s*.

to plan	
I plan	we plan
you plan	you plan
he, she it plans	they plan

I *plan* to call in an internet marketing expert.
You *plan* very productive meeting agendas.
We *plan* our marketing strategy a year in advance.
Arthur *plans* his report before writing it.
The company *plans* to review our benefits package.
They *plan* to increase our company's exposure in China.

IRREGULARS

Many irregular verbs also change form in third person singular, present tense.

to do	
I do	we do
you do	you do
he, she it does	they do

Mr. Tanka *does* business internationally.
Ometraco's affiliates *do* business internationally.

to have	
I have	we have
you have	you have
he, she it has	they have

I *have* five years of experience in my field.
She *has* ten years of experience in her field.
Lilly Woo *has* ten years of experience in her field.

to be	
I am	we are
you are	you are
he, she it is	they are

I *am* a salesperson.
He *is* a sales manager.
Aldo *is* a sales manager.
Ometraco *is* a strong company.
We *are* working the new territory together.
You *are* an asset to the company.
They *are* the company's top salespeople.

Notice the *I am*. To be is the only verb in English that changes form in the first person singular.

Factual Present

Present tense verbs relate not only present time or condition, but they also relate truths, facts that do not change with time.

> A circle *is* round.
> The earth *revolves* around the sun.
> Hope *springs* eternal.*
> Winter in New York *is* cold.

The present tense relates that winter in New York is cold when the writer is relating that fact in December, but the present tense also states that fact (as a truth) when spoken in spring or in fall. Winter is *always* cold in New York.

Tense in Writing Directions or Documentation

For the business writer, **factual present** is particularly useful for giving directions or for writing documentation:

> When the user *presses* Shift-Command T, a screen *appears*, and the user then *selects* the tab settings that *appear* on the final document.

Even though it is true that later, in the future, when the user gives the command, the screen *will appear* (future tense), the screen *always* appears when the user gives this command. Because the fact is *always* true, present tense can be used instead of future. Notice that the verb *to appear* is also used in the present tense.

As a stylistic device, present tense is stronger, more direct, and more quickly understood by the reader than any other tense. All those qualities make the factual present a useful choice for documentation writing.

---

hope springs eternal—Even in difficult circumstances, people hope for the best.

Simplify directions even more by giving them in second person present tense. When giving a direction or command, omit the pronoun *you*, which is understood.

(You) Press Shift-Command T. A screen appears.
(You) Select tab settings that appear on the final document.

Referencing Data

Analysts and scientific writers also use the simple present tense to reference figures, charts, or tables, or in supporting text.

These figures **show**…[present tense; not *showed*, past tense]

Even though you may be reporting a completed experiment, the figures are factual and still show the same thing they showed at the moment of completion.

The table below **indicates**   [not future tense, *will indicate*]

Even though the reader hasn't yet read the table, the table is factual and always indicates the same thing in the past, present, and in the future.

Survey respondents **report** that they **refer** most drug-related questions to the primary care physicians.

It's Your Turn

Exercise 1

Underline the most accurate verbs (past or present) to complete the following paragraph.

During last week's interview, the operations manager (said, says) that he always (submitted, submits) the monthly report by the second Tuesday of the month. We (check, checked) the records, which (showed, show) that, although he (submitted, submits) the January, February, and March reports on time, he (completed, completes) the monthly reports later every month.

PRESENT CONTINUOUS

Continuous, or "progressive," verbs end in *ing* (the present participle) and are used with a form of the verb to be.

José *is calculating* the interest now.

The form of *to be* tells whether the verb is present—*José **is** calculating the interest*—or past—*José **was** calculating the interest.* The continuous is meant to show activity that is continuing through a period of time and *is of limited duration.* In its simplest version, the **present continuous shows activity that is continuing right through this present moment.** *(José **is** now calculating the interest.)*

ESL writers often use the present continuous when the simple present correctly shows factual or customary habitual status.

Incorrect: The browser *is freezing* every time I open the editing panel. (present continuous)

Correct: The browser *freezes* every time I open the editing panel. (factual, customary, present tense)

When people ask *Where **do** you **work**?* they are asking for a fact, for your habitual occupation. The question *Where **are** you **working**?* is also commonly used to ask for your habitual occupation. The habitual, factual present response:

I work at First Connecticut Savings.

It is, of course, possible that you will not always be working there; where you are working may have recently changed or may be about to change. Your response to this question may use present continuous to include a temporary, ongoing activity (a "period of limited duration").

I *am working* at a golf course for the summer.
[This answer will change with the season.]

I *am working* in the city this week.   *or*
I *am working* in New York through the weekend.
[This present, ongoing activity is likely to change.]

Compare the following present continuous (a) and simple present (b) sentences.

1. a. Susan *is reviewing* your application. [now]

    b. Susan *reviews* all applications. [always]

2. a. Several of the trustees *are writing* articles.
        [for this publication]

    b. Several of the trustees *write* articles. [regularly]

3. a. Mr. Yung *is following* the required procedure.
        [for this project]

    b. Mr. Yung *follows* the required procedures.
        [for all projects, habitually]

The present tense (2nd sentence) in the examples above indicates actions that are generally true (factual present) and are, in that sense, ongoing. Fill in the blanks below with the correct form of *review*.

1. I _____ credit requests regularly.

2. I _____ several credit requests today.

The first sentence in the simple present indicates an activity that occurs on a regular basis. The second sentence, in the present continuous, indicates an activity going on today, within a specific time frame.

AWKWARD USAGE

We have English verbs that describe a *state of being*. These verbs include words such as *to see, know, be, appear, believe, feel, mean, need, remember, understand,* and *want*. In most cases, we do not use the continuous form of these verbs. Here are incorrect and corrected uses of the verbs.

Incorrect: I *am knowing* the committee members.
Correct: I *know* the committee members.

Incorrect   I *am needing* more time.
Correct: I *need* more time.

Incorrect: I *am being* a scientist.
Correct: I *am* a scientist.

IT'S YOUR TURN

EXERCISE 2

First, underline the complete verb form in each sentence, then identify each as present or present continuous. Change incorrect uses of the present continuous tense to simple present.

1.   Many tellers are wanting a raise.

2.   The maintenance department is working during this shutdown.

3.   Our catalogue department processes orders throughout the holiday season.

4.   I am enclosing samples in this letter.

5.   Our group writes the company's grant proposals.

6.   His client is owning the subsidiary.

7.   I am believing his version of the incident.

The Time Was Then—Past Tense

The past tense of regular verbs is usually formed by adding a -*d* or an -*ed* ending. Although you cannot always hear it when native English speakers say it, the ending is necessary to show past tense in writing. It is most difficult to distinguish the spoken -ed ending when the word that follows begins with a *d* or *t*. In speech, sometimes two sounds that are close together like *d* and *t* (*closed title*) are blurred, and the verb's *-ed* ending slides into the word that follows.

I closed title on that house yesterday.
I closed down the program before I inserted the disk.

closed title   *sounds like:*   close title
closed down   *sounds like:*   close down

Native speakers may blend these double consonant sounds so that the *-ed* sound is not pronounced at all. Although -ed endings sound like *-ed*, *-d*, or *-t*, they are *written* as *ed*. Even though the listener cannot always hear or distinguish the *-ed*, it must be written.

Three rules to remember: When adding -ed to a verb:

1. Words ending in *t* or *d*, pronounce -*ed* as a syllable.

written as	sounds like
deposited	deposited (id)
compounded	compounded (id)

2. Words ending in: *p, f, s, sh, ch, k,* and soft *th* sound as though they end in -t.

walked	walk(t)
reached	reach(t)

3. Words ending in: *b, m, w, v, z, n, l, r, j, y, g* and hard *th* sound as though they end in -d.

designed	design(d)
reviewed	review(d)

IRREGULAR PAST TENSE VERBS

Rather than adding an ending, some irregular verbs change form completely in the past tense, and some do not change at all. Following are examples of some of the most often-used irregular verbs and their past tense forms.

be	was, were	see	saw	speak	spoke
have	had	write	wrote	drive	drove
do	did	read	read	say	said
go	went	lead	led	know	knew
quit	quit	think	thought	put	put
arise	arose	forgive	forgave	see	saw
know	knew	get	got	give	gave

It is important to memorize irregular verbs in the past form. Most grammar books and all dictionaries list irregular past tense forms of the verb. These resources group them in sections that make them easier to remember, eg. past tense verbs ending in *ght* or verbs that do not change. One good resource book is *Grammar in Plain English,* by Harriet Diamond and Phyllis Dutwin (published by Barron's Educational Series).

IDIOMATIC INDICATION OF THE PAST

Another way a writer can indicate a past action is by using the phrase *used to…* with the base form of the verb.

> Credit Lyonnais *used to* hold that mortgage.
> Regulations *used to* require two signatures.
> I *used to* teach computer technology.

THE TIME IS YET TO COME— FUTURE TENSE

The future tense uses *will* or *shall* with the base form of the verb. Example: *Henry **will drive** tomorrow.*

W*ill* is more common than *shall*.

> I *will* go with you.
> All the directors *will* resign.
> We *will* resign.

I will (or shall) review	we will (or shall) review
you will review	you will review
he (she, it) will review	they will review

IDIOMATIC INDICATIONS OF FUTURE

Another way to express future time is to use the phrase *is going to* with the base form.

> He *is going to* play tennis on Sunday.
> The movie *is going to* end at six.
> We *are going to* speak later.
> The company *is going to* close.

Finally, Americans express future tense by using the present continuous verb with a specific future time reference within the sentence:

> He *is singing* next week.
> I *am working* overtime tomorrow.

IT'S YOUR TURN

Exercise 3

Underline the most appropriate verb form to convey the precise time for each sentence. Indicate whether it is present tense, present continuous, or future tense.

1. I (will enclose, will be enclosing) a rate sheet when I mail the proposal.

2. His inspections (are, are being) meticulous.

3. If I (am leading, lead), I can cut back on campaign appearances during the final month.

4. Throughout the next four months, the committee (reviews, will review, is reviewing) all proposals.

5. Even though I know he will not agree, I (am considering, consider) him the best designer.

6. The temporary employees (pack, will pack, are packing) the fifty orders that we plan to ship tonight.

7. I (am, am being) a computer technician.

8. The business plan, written last year, (outlines, will outline) the company's plans for the future.

9. I (run, am running) for office.

10. Thomas (likes, is liking) his new position.

EXERCISE I

During last week's interview, the operations manager <u>said</u> that he always <u>submits</u> the monthly report by the second Tuesday of the month. We <u>checked</u> the records, which <u>show</u> that, although he <u>submitted</u> the January, February, and March reports on time, last quarter he <u>completed</u> the monthly reports later every month.

EXERCISE 2

1. *rewrite:* Many tellers <u>want</u> a raise. (present)
2. The maintenance department <u>is working</u> during this shutdown. (present continuous)
3. Our catalogue department <u>processes</u> orders throughout the holiday season. (present)
4. *rewrite*: I <u>enclose</u> samples in this letter. (present)
5. Our group <u>writes</u> the company's grant proposals. (present)
6. *rewrite:* His client <u>owns</u> the subsidiary. (present)
7. *rewrite:* I <u>believe</u> his version of the incident. (present)

EXERCISE 3

1. I <u>will enclose</u> a rate sheet when I mail the proposal. (future tense)
2. His inspections <u>are</u> meticulous. (present tense)
3. If I <u>am leading</u>, I can cut back on campaign appearances during the final month. (present continuous)
4. Throughout the next four months, the committee <u>will review</u> all proposals. (future tense)
5. Even though I know he will not agree, I <u>consider</u> him the best designer. (present tense)
6. The temporary employees <u>will pack</u> the fifty orders that we plan to ship tonight. (future tense, if the employees have not yet begun to pack)

or

The temporary employees <u>are packing</u> the fifty orders that we plan to ship tonight. (present continuous, if the employees have begun to pack and are still packing)

ANSWER KEY

7. I <u>am</u> a computer technician. (present tense)
8. The business plan, written last year, <u>outlines</u> the company's plans for the future. (present tense)
9. I <u>am running</u> for office.   (present continuous tense)
10.Thomas <u>likes</u> his new position. (present tense)

Other Tense Issues

6

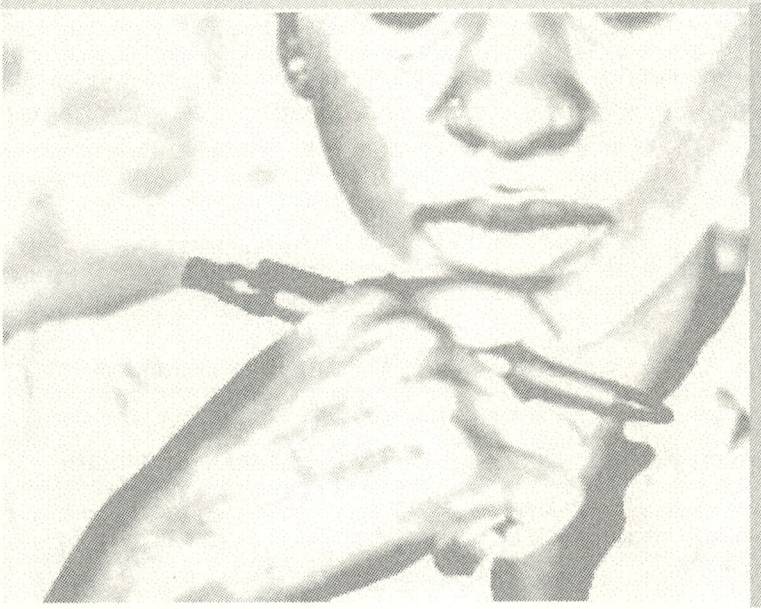

WHAT MAKES A TENSE PERFECT? A LITTLE HELP!

The present perfect tense describes actions that began in the past and continue up to and into the present and, most likely, the future. Perfect tenses are easy to recognize because they all use a form of the helping verb *to have: has, have,* or *had.*

Past	I *wrote* 20 years ago.
Present Perfect	I *have written* for more than 20 years.
Present	I *write* today.
Past	John *started* working for Diamond Drum Corporation in 1998.
Present Perfect	John *has worked* for Diamond Drum for twenty years.
Present	John still *works* for Diamond Drum today.
Past	Fei *worked* at Rainbow Corp. for six years.
Present Perfect	Fei *has worked* at Sun Inc. for two years.
Present	Fei works at Sun Inc.

LOOK FOR SIGNALS

Certain prepositions are used idiomatically in partnership with certain tenses. Such prepositions are "signal" words that direct you to the correct verb form.

If your sentence uses *since, by, beginning in, from,* or some other phrase that anchors the beginning of the activity in the past, a perfect tense is called for.

Examples:

1. Marie *has developed* four major projects *since* (not *from*) the beginning of the first quarter. [present perfect tense]
2. The company *has been enjoying* a tax holiday since (not *from*) 2004 [progressive/present perfect]
3. Max *has worked* at Flint Tech *for* (not *since*) twelve years. [present perfect]
4. Our relationship with ICU, Inc. *started in* (not *since*) 2002. [simple past; a single point in time]

Since signals an activity that began at a specific point in time and continues to the present or one that has been completed.

Incorrect:	I *was* using the current system *since* 2006.
Correct:	I *have been using* the current system *since* 2006.

Incorrect:	The company *is* in business *since* 1990.
Correct:	The company *has been* in business *since* 1990.

For signals a total amount of time; a duration.
By and *in* signal a single point in time, either past or future.
Before signals a single point in time.

The **past perfect tense** describes a past action that occurred at a specific point prior to another specific past point in time:

PAST PERFECT   SIGNAL   PAST
I **had written** for 20 years *before* my books **became** best sellers.

PAST PERFECT   SIGNAL   PAST
John **had finished** all the trial preparation *before* Lin **joined** the defense team.

PAST PERFECT   SIGNAL   SIGNAL
We **had discussed** a merger *before* OBE's *recent* scandal.

⌨ IT'S YOUR TURN

EXERCISE 1

Underline the correct signal word for each sentence.

1. Mr. Habib has been our customer (from, since) 1999.

2. All capital expenses are frozen (from, since) today through the end of the second quarter.

3. Anton has been developing our personnel policy manual (since, by) March.

The **future perfect tense** is used to describe a future action that will occur *before* another future action.

SIGNAL	FUTURE	FUTURE PERFECT

By the time my books **become** best sellers, **I will have been** writing for 20 years.

This type of sentence also works in reverse.

I will have been writing for 20 years *by the time* my books **become** best sellers.

Fei **will have worked** for Sun Inc. for six years *by* 2012.

SIMPLE AND PERFECT TENSE FORMS OF THE VERB *TO SIGN*

They *sign* the contract every year.	(present)
They *have signed* all the contracts.	(present perfect)
Jonathan *has* always *signed* contracts for his company.	(present perfect)

> Note: It is correct to insert a modifier, such as always, between the helping word and the verb.

He *signed* the contract at 10:00 a.m.   (past)

He *had* already *signed* it before I arrived.   (past perfect)

The Morgans *had signed* the contracts before
the attorney reviewed them.   (past perfect)

I *will sign* that contract after you leave.   (future)

I *will have signed* it by the time you return.   (future perfect)

They *will have signed* it by tomorrow.   (future perfect)

> Notice the shift in helping verbs. *Has* works only with
> *he, she, it* (or names) in the present perfect. In the
> past perfect, *had* always works, with no exceptions.
> In the future perfect, *will* is used, with no exceptions.

PERFECT TENSE

Regular verbs (like *to sign* or *to work*) use the same form for
the past and past perfect tenses, adding a past tense form of
the auxiliary verb *to have* for past perfect. Past tense verbs are
often spelled the same as past participle forms.

Present	Past	Past Participle
		(used with helping words)
work	worked	worked
develop	developed	developed
sign	signed	signed

The examples for present perfect tense on page 116 use an
irregular verb, *wrote*. Many irregular verbs change form to create the past and past participle.

Present	Past	Past Participle
		(used with helping words)
write	wrote	written
become	became	become
be	was/were	been
get	got	gotten

SIMPLE AND PERFECT TENSE FORMS
OF THE VERB *TO BE*

The most often used verb in English is *to be*; it is irregular.
Take a moment to review the way *to be* changes from simple to
perfect tenses.

I *am* a web designer now.	(present)
I *have been* a web designer since 2001.	(present perfect)
He *has been* a web designer for six years.	(present perfect)
I *was* a web designer a year ago.	(past)
He *was* web designer three years ago.	(past)
I *had been* a photo editor for two years before I changed careers.	(past perfect)
He *had been* an accountant for thirty years before he retired.	(past perfect)
I *will be* a production artist when I pass the exam.	(future)
She *will have been* a web designer for six months by the time she gets her degree.	(future perfect)

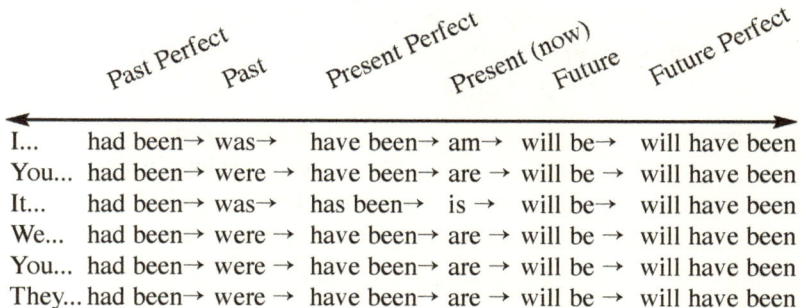

Past Perfect	Past	Present Perfect	Present (now)	Future	Future Perfect
I... had been→	was→	have been→	am→	will be→	will have been
You... had been→	were →	have been→	are →	will be →	will have been
It... had been→	was→	has been→	is →	will be→	will have been
We... had been→	were →	have been→	are →	will be →	will have been
You... had been→	were →	have been→	are →	will be →	will have been
They... had been→	were →	have been→	are →	will be →	will have been

IRREGULAR VERB *TO KNOW*

I... had known→knew→have known→know→will know→will have known
You...had known→knew→have known→know→will know→will have known
He, she, it... had known→knew→have known→knows→will know→
will have known
We... had known→knew→have known→know→will know→will have known
You... had known→knew→have known→know→will know→will have known
They... had known→knew→have known→know→will know→will have known

IT'S YOUR TURN

EXERCISE 2

Select the correct from of the verb *to know* for each of the following sentences.

1. I _____ the director. [today, factual]

2. I _____ the director when he worked at Selpats. [a single point in time past]

3. I _____ the director for twelve years. [from a time in the past and continuing today]

4. I _____ the director for eight years before he retired. [at a time in the past, prior to another time that is being referred to by the writer (or speaker)]

5. I _____ the director after this luncheon. [in the future]

6. I _____ the director for six years by the time he retires. [from a time in the past to a specific time in the future]

Notice how the tenses in the following paragraph relate to each other in the time frame of the activities being described.

Even before he *submitted* the proposal, Emad *had realized* its flaws. He *has written* a number of proposals, but the budget in this one *is* a problem. He *expects* to receive a two-week extension. He *will rewrite* the budget. By the time he resubmits this proposal, it *will have taken* one month to complete.

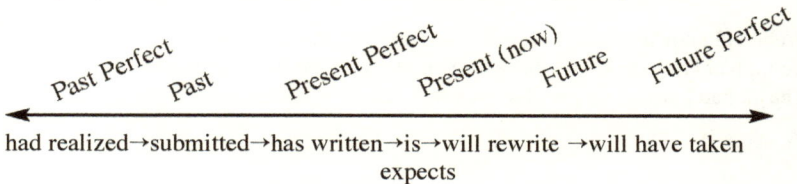

Past Perfect   Past   Present Perfect   Present (now)   Future   Future Perfect

←——→

had realized→submitted→has written→is→will rewrite →will have taken
expects

💻 IT'S YOUR TURN

EXERCISE 3

Underline or highlight the correct form of the verb in each sentence.

We (need, are needing, have needed) this report for a long time. George (prepares, prepared, had prepared) it last week, but (forgot, had forgotten, forgets) to send it to Mr. Medina for review. Mr. Medina (reviews, has reviewed, had reviewed) [as of today, right now, this afternoon] most of the support material, and this morning [earlier than now] he (asked, has asked, is asking) for George's report. Tell George to send it immediately.

PERFECT CONTINUOUS TENSE

The **perfect continuous tense** has a known beginning point in the past, continues into the present, and may continue through the present and into the future. This tense is built by joining the continuous form and the perfect form.

Continuous	=	*to be*	+	**present participle**
Present continuous	=	I am		planning (to go).
Past continuous	=	I was		planning (to go before the storm warning).

Perfect	=	*to have*	+	**past participle**
Present continuous	=	I have		planned.
Past continuous	=	I had		planned.

Perfect Continuous = to have + *to be* + **present participle**

Present perfect				
continuous	=	I have	been	planning.
Past perfect				
continuous	=	I had	been	planning.
Future perfect				
continuous	=	I (will) have	been planning.	

Present perfect continuous: I *have been running* since 3:00.

Past perfect continuous: I *had been running* next to Sean until he dropped out of the race.

Future perfect continuous: I *will have been running* for forty minutes by the time I reach the four-mile mark.

The last example sentence also works in reverse.

By the time I reach the four-mile mark, I *will have been running* for forty minutes.

Reverse these sentences:

By the time we finish this analysis, the study *will have been running* for twenty years.

Chang *has been directing* the study since Tom's retirement.

🖥 IT'S YOUR TURN

EXERCISE 4

Underline the complete verb forms in each sentence; then identify the tenses.

1. Ever since the audit, accounting has been posting expenses.
2. Since our price cut, sales have been increasing.
3. When we get a purchase order, we begin the invoice process.
4. This bank has requested a charter.
5. We expect to pass the approval process.

🖥 IT'S YOUR TURN

EXERCISE 5

Fill in each blank with the correct form of the verb. The words in italics will help you determine the correct tense.

1. (acquire) No long-term debt _____ by the company *since* 2000.

2. (be) *Last* quarter earnings _____ higher than predicted.

3. (start) Three of the four divisions _____ commercial applications *in* 2000.

4. (be) The group has established a new factory in Thailand that _____ fully operational *by* 2012.

5. (bank) The company _____ with us *since* last October.

SHIFTING TENSES

When a writer wants to convey specific time differences within a single paragraph, the writer must shift tenses.

> We *have been seeing* this particular error message ever since we installed the newest software version, although *we had occasionally seen* the same message with the original version.

These verb form changes relate specific time meanings to the software users who are trying to isolate the cause of their technical problem. Changing the verb form shows a high level of language mastery. It also gives precise information in very few words. Again, verb form mastery leads to concise style.

🖥 IT'S YOUR TURN

EXERCISE 6

In the banker's XYZ Loan Request on page 126, all the verb tenses are used correctly. Perfect tenses are often signaled by other words in the sentence, such as *on, by,* or *since.* In such sentences, the signal words are in italics. The verbs are in bold.

Part A: First, read the entire call report, noticing how the tenses shift to convey different times.

Part B: Starting on page 127, each paragraph is reprinted and numbered and followed by a timeline. Verbs are in bold in each paragraph on the timeline. The first two paragraphs are done for you; use these as guidelines.

Part A

Subject: XYZ Loan Request
Date: May 1, 2007

1. I **called** Mr. Xin *on* April 20, 2007, and he **said** that his company, XYZ, **needs** a new $4 million line to expand. XYZ **produces** surveillance equipment.

2. XYZ **has been producing** home security systems *since* 1996 and *by* 2003 was one of the top three selling manufacturers in the country. It **had** even **surpassed** the long-time industry giant HIT. But in response to wide-scale security threats, the company **has been scaling** down its home security division and **has been providing** security equipment for public venues. *By* the end of this year, it **will have fulfilled** contracts with three major metropolitan areas with surveillance-equipped street signs.

3. This loan **will enable** XYZ to expand its existing factories. That expansion **is scheduled** for completion *by* the end of 2008. XYZ **expects** to triple its output of city-designed surveillance equipment and, if construction **finishes** on schedule, XYZ **will be** the largest manufacturer of surveillance signs in the country. *By* that time, it **will have** completely **closed** its residential branch and **will be** exclusively **working** with government contracts, producing surveillance-equipped street signs, commercial signs, and billboards.

4. I **said** that I **expected** our bank to meet all of XYZ's needs. XYZ **is** a valuable client and our relationship **has** always **been** profitable. I **have enclosed**, with this report, a credit history and XYZ's profit projections.

5. I told Mr. Xin that we **will prepare** documents for his review. He **is waiting** for our next call.

Part B

Paragraph 1:

I **called** Mr. Xin *on* April 20, 2007, and he **said** that his company, XYZ, **needs** a new $4 million line to expand. XYZ **produces** surveillance equipment.

Past		Present	
April 20, 2007		May 1, 2007	
called		needs	
said		produces	

Paragraph 2:

XYZ **has been producing** home security systems *since* 1996 and *by* 2003 was one of the top three selling manufacturers in the country. It **had** even **surpassed** the long-time industry giant HIT. But in response to wide-scale security threats, the company **has been scaling** down its home security division and **has been providing** security equipment for public venues. *By* the end of this year, it **will have fulfilled** contracts with three major metropolitan areas with surveillance-equipped street signs.

Past Perfect	Past	Present Perfect Continuous	Present	Future Perfect
1989	2003	since 1989	May 1,	end of this year
had surpassed	was	has been producing	2007	will have doubled
		has been scaling		
		has been providing		

Paragraph 3:

This loan **will enable** XYZ to expand its existing factories. That expansion **is scheduled** for completion *by* the end of 2007. XYZ **expects** to triple its output of city-designed surveillance equipment and, if construction **finishes** on schedule, XYZ **will be** the largest manufacturer of surveillance signs in the country. *By* that time, it **will have** completely **closed** its residential branch and **will be** exclusively **working** with government contracts, producing surveillance-equipped street signs, commercial signs, and billboards.

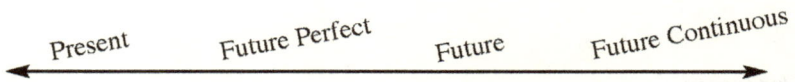

Present   Future Perfect   Future   Future Continuous
←——→

Paragraph 4:

I **said** that I **expected** our bank to meet all of XYZ's needs. XYZ **is** a valuable client and our relationship **has** always **been** profitable. I **have enclosed**, with this report, a credit history and XYZ's profit projections.

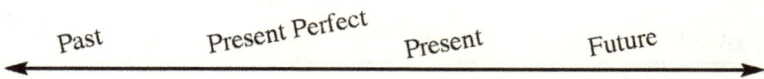

Past   Present Perfect   Present   Future
←——→

Paragraph 5:

I told Mr. Xin that we **will prepare** documents for his review. He **is waiting** for our next call.

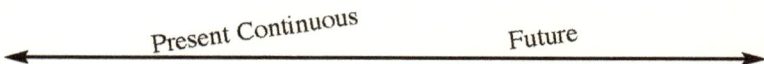

Present Continuous   Future
←——→

THE MODAL CONNECTION

English tenses build on these forms by adding auxiliary words that extend the verb's ability to indicate precise time or conditional nuances in the sentence. Some auxiliary words indicate time or intention without changing tense form. Such auxiliaries are called **modals**:

can	will	might
may	must	should
shall	could	would

You have already been working with two modals: *will* and *shall*, which are used with the base form of the verb to indicate future tense. Other modals follow the same model as *will* and *shall*. While these two modals show tense, most are used to convey other, more subtle meanings, as you will see in the next section. (Modals *never* change form to show tense.)

Modals are used with the "basic building block" verb forms: base, infinitive, and present participle.

Base:	work	hold	review
Infinitive:	to work	to hold	to review
Present Participle	working	holding	reviewing

Modals and Meaning

Modals add a shade of meaning to the verb. That meaning varies depending upon the modal chosen and the context. A modal can indicate the writer's attitude or opinion concerning the action, or it may indicate a level of probability. A modal conveys precise meaning in a subtle, concise way.

1. A modal demonstrates attitude.

Modals affect the tone of a request or response to a request. Some convey the same basic meaning, but different attitudes. Consider the difference between *can* and *could* and *will* and *would* in a request. The meaning is the same, but *could* and *would* are considered more polite, less forceful. It's a subtle difference between *Can you bring those figures to the next meeting?* and the more polite *Could you bring those figures to the next meeting?* The following example shows how using the modal makes your writing more concise.

> modal: *could* *Could* you send documentation for this research?
>
> rather than   I would appreciate it if you would send documentation for this research.

2. A modal assures of something or someone's ability.

Another important subtlety is the use of the modal *can* to assure the reader of ability. *Can* emphatically states the ability to do something. *Can* is the only modal that can be used in this way.

> modal: *can*   You *can* help me with this design.
> rather than   You are able to help me with this design.

What's the difference between *Can you match the competitor's price?* and *Will you match the competitor's price?*

Can you match the competitor's price? is a straightforward question of **capability**; *Will you match the competitor's price?* is a straightforward question of **intent**.

Could you match the competitor's price? or *Would you match the competitor's price?* are more polite requests that are open to many possible reasons for declining to match the price. Those reasons may or may not relate to your ability or desire to do so.

If the written reply to the request above uses the ambiguous *could* or *would*, that writer would be required to offer an explanation for meeting or not meeting the price.

a. I *could* match the price, *but not the deadline.*

b. I *could* meet the price *if I used the same supplier for construction materials.*

Could and *would* generally imply the ability to do something under certain conditions.

3. A modal shows opinion.

| modal: *should* | The owner *should* listen to her employees. |
| rather than | I believe it is important that the owner listen to her employees. |

4. A modal indicates a level of importance or intensity.

| modal: *must* | The trainees *must* attend every session. |
| rather than | It is necessary that the trainees attend every session. |

These two sentences mean the same thing; both are grammatically correct. The first sentence, however, reflects modern business style, and for meaning it depends on the modal *must*. It uses the simple base form of the verb, *attend*.

Must is an emphatic command. It is a strong modal, leaving no doubt in the reader's mind that it is *necessary* to attend. Consider the difference in the level of importance if the writer used *could* or *may* in place of *must*.

Modals that indicate *levels* of importance or intensity are *can, could, may, might, should, and must.*

5. A modal indicates permission.

May indicates permission. *Can* has been used incorrectly used in place of *may* for so long it has become an acceptable idiomatic usage in spoken English. In writing, however, many people prefer the old style. This, too, is changing over time, but the correct formal request for permission is still *may*.

| modal: *may* | *May* I publish your findings in my report? |
| rather than | Can I publish your findings in my report? |

6. A modal gives advice.

Should is used to advise, to say that someone ought to do something.

modal: *should*	Trainees *should attend* every session.
rather than	It is advisable that trainees attend every session.

Again, the two sentences mean the same thing, but the first is preferable because it is concise.

Other modals that advise are *can, could, may,* and *might.*

7. A modal indicates degree of possibility.

Degrees of possibility range from **may**, which indicates that an action is **possible**, to **must**, indicating an **almost positive prediction**, to **will**, which indicates absolute **certainty**.

modal: *must*	This vague language *must* cause confusion.
rather than	This vague language is most certainly the cause of much confusion.

Other modals that indicate degree of possibility are *can, could, may, might, should,* and *will.*

▤ IT'S YOUR TURN

EXERCISE 7

Try each modal, one by one, in the sentences below. Each one makes a correct sentence grammatically. Compare the changes in meaning as the modal changes.

1. _____ I review the figures on the MIK account?
   a. Could   c. Might
   b. May   d Should

2. You _____ close stores to improve the bottom line.
   a. could   c. must
   b. should   d. will

3. Our company _____ be bought out.
   a. could   d. should
   b. might   e. must
   c. may   f. will

IT'S YOUR TURN

EXERCISE 8

Use the modals below to complete the following sentences.

should   will   can   must   might

1. **Possibility:**
   Maria _____ ask for that promotion.

2. **The writer's prediction or advice about her asking:**
   Maria _____ ask for that promotion.

3. **A demand that she ask:**
   Maria _____ ask for that promotion.

4. **A belief that the action will surely take place:**
   Maria _____ ask for that promotion.

5. **A belief that she is able to ask:**
   Maria _____ ask for that promotion.

⌨ IT'S YOUR TURN

EXERCISE 9

Each numbered sentence below contains one or two modals.
After each sentence, write your own sentence using the same
modal (or modals) with the verb (or verbs) in parentheses.
The first one is done for you.

1. If I **could** find an investor, I **would** create software for
   online auctions. (*could*: used to express ability eg. technical
   or financial; *would*: used to express a desire)

   (retire, learn) *If I could retire, I would learn to sail.*

2. The company **should** revise the old dress code.
   (used as strong advice)

   (consider) _____.

3. The policy **should** be effective by January.
   (used to predict future events)

   (be) _____.

4. The claims adjuster **must** enter the ID number in the correct
   field. (used as an emphatic command)

   (attend) _____.

5. Faulty data entry **must** be the cause of that accounting error.
   (used to express an almost positive prediction)

   (affect) _____.

6. Employees **may** open 401(K) plans if they want to. (used to
   express permission)

   (send) _____.

7. The election **may** be close. (used to express possibility)

   (go) _____.

8. If we **can** double sales this year, we **will** break the record for sales in this region. (*can*: used to express ability; *will*: used to express future—note that the use of *if* changes *will* to a *possible* future).

    (complete; be) _____

    _____.

By choosing the correct modal, the writer is able to convey varying degrees of probability (*might, may, should, will*) or to report progressively more emphatic directives (*could, may, should, can, must*). Use modals very carefully to convey the tone you really want to project when you write.

So far we have used modals in their simplest forms. They can also be used in passive tenses (*can* also *be used*; the trials *will be concluded* on time) and in perfect tenses (W*e would have corrected* it if we had known; he *might have filed it*). Often, modals appear in passive perfect form (She *should have been told* about the merger).

SUBJUNCTIVES

The subjunctive clause begins with "that" and delivers a demand or explains a requirement. "That" introduces a noun clause. The entire clause is used as a noun and the verb in this clause is *always* the base form. **Even if the subject is third person singular**, it is followed by the **base form** of the verb, *not* **the infinitive** (to + verb), *not* **present tense**.

The base form never changes in a subjunctive clause.

  He demanded *that the issue **be** closed*. [not *is* closed]
  Her boss insisted *that she **work** on Saturdays*. [not she ***works***]
  Requirements specified *that bids **be** in writing*. [not bids ***are***]
  The contract requires *that an attorney **be** present*. [not *is*]
  The contract requires *that they **be** present*. [not ***are***]

If Clauses—Conditions, Hopes, and Wishes

Conditional clauses present another exception for the irregular verb *to be*: *Was* is the past tense form of the verb *to be* for first (I) and third (he, she, it) person singular—*except* when expressing a wish, a hope, or a condition contrary to fact.

Example: *If* I *could* retire early, I *would.*

When expressing a wish or a condition that is contrary to fact (If I *were* a rich man), we use *were* as the form of the verb *to be.* Such sentences typically include the words *wish* or *if.*

Examples: *If* you *were* the candidate, we could win.
He *wishes* he *were* more trusted by the board.

Following are comparisons of sentences expressing either a fact, a wish, or a condition contrary to fact. Notice the use of *were* in the second example in each set.

fact: The book is online as a free download; therefore, I do not have to buy it.

condition: *If* the book *were* not available as a free download, I would buy it.

fact: I am not the manger; I cannot give you credit.
condition: *If* I *were* the manager, I would give you credit.

IT'S YOUR TURN

Exercise 10

Choose the correct verb form in these sentences.

1. I wish I (was, were) the director of this project.

2. Thomas (was, were) a manager before the reorganization.

3. When Sylvia left, she (was, were) ready for a change.

4. If he (was, were) in charge, he would give us the account.

5. We wished the bid (was, were) lower.

EXERCISE 1
1. Mr. Habib has been our customer <u>since</u> 1999.
2. All capital expenses are frozen <u>from</u> today through the end of the second quarter.
3. Anton has been developing our personnel policy manual <u>since</u> March.

EXERCISE 2
1. I <u>know</u> the director.
2. I <u>knew</u> the director when he worked at Selpats.
3. I <u>have known</u> the director for twelve years.
4. I <u>had known</u> the director before he retired.
5. I <u>will know</u> the director after this luncheon.
6. I <u>will have known</u> the director for six years by the time he retires.

EXERCISE 3
We <u>have needed</u> this report for a long time. George <u>had prepared</u> it last week, but <u>forgot</u> to send it to Mr. Medina for review. Mr. Medina <u>has reviewed</u> [as of today, right now, afternoon] most of the support material, and this morning [earlier than now] he <u>asked</u> for George's report. Tell George to send it immediately.

EXERCISE 4
1. Ever since the audit, accounting <u>has been posting</u> expenses. (present perfect continuous)
2. Since our price cut, sales <u>have been increasing</u>. (present perfect continuous)
3. When we get a purchase order, we <u>begin</u> the invoice process. (present)
4. This bank <u>has requested</u> a charter. (present perfect)
5. We <u>expect</u> to pass the approval process. (present)

EXERCISE 5
1. No long-term debt <u>has been acquired</u> by the company *since* 2000. (present perfect continuous)

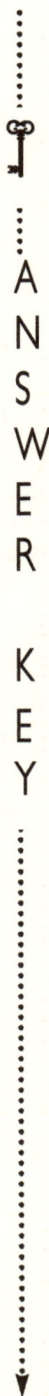

A
N
S
W
E
R

K
E
Y

2. *Last* quarter earnings <u>were</u> higher than predicted.   (past)
3. Three of the four divisions <u>started</u> commercial applications in 2000.   (past)
5. The group has established a new factory in Thailand that <u>will be</u> fully operational by 2012.   (future)
6. The company <u>has been banking</u> with us since last October.   (present perfect continuous)

EXERCISE 6

Paragraph 3

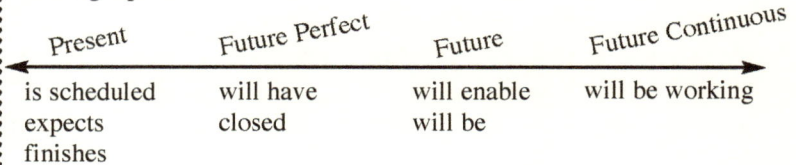

Present	Future Perfect	Future	Future Continuous
is scheduled	will have	will enable	will be working
expects	closed	will be	
finishes			

Paragraph 4

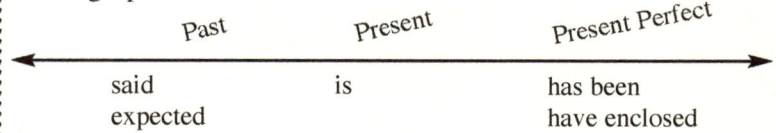

Past	Present	Present Perfect
said	is	has been
expected		have enclosed

Paragraph 5

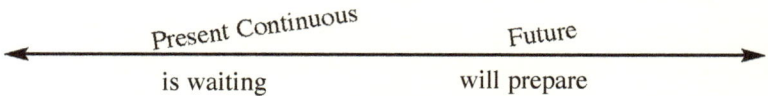

Present Continuous	Future
is waiting	will prepare

EXERCISE 7

1. _____ I review the figures on the MIK account?
   - a. could: asks permission.
   - b. may: asks permission.
   - c. might: asks permission. (less common).
   - d. should: asks if "I" ought to review the figures.
2. You _____ close stores to improve the bottom line.
   - a. could: is a suggestion.
   - b. should: is a strong suggestion.
   - c. must: is an emphatic instruction.
   - d. will: states the *fact* that the stores will close; it has been decided.
3. Our company _____ be bought out.
   - a. could: indicates that the possibility exists; there may be rumors.
   - b. might: indicates that the possibility exists; there may be rumors.
   - c. may: indicates that the possibility exists; there may be rumors.
   - d. should: states my opinion.
   - e. must: strongly states my opinion.
   - f. will: states that a buyout is imminent; it is going to occur.

EXERCISE 8

1. might
2. should
3. must
4. will
5. can

EXERCISE 9

Possible answers:
2. Your <u>should</u> consider working from home.
3. Our new policy <u>should</u> be in place by January.
4. All managers <u>must</u> attend the online seminar.
5. The layoffs <u>must</u> affect morale.

6. Team members <u>may</u> send articles for the next company newsletter to me by May 15.
7. I <u>may</u> go to the conference this year.
8. If we <u>can</u> complete this report, we <u>will</u> be finished for the day.

EXERCISE 10

1. I wish I <u>were</u> the director of this project.
2. Thomas <u>was</u> a manager before the reorganization.
3. When Sylvia left, she <u>was</u> ready for a change.
4. If he <u>were</u> vice president, he would give us the account.
5. We wished the bid <u>were</u> lower.

7

Translations That Just Won't Work

- ➤ SELECTING THE RIGHT WORD FORM
- ➤ PARTICIPLES
- ➤ NOUN MISFITS
- ➤ INFINITIVES OF PURPOSE
- ➤ NOUNS THAT NEVER CHANGE

SELECTING THE RIGHT WORD FORM

As you search for just the right word, you will find that some words defy translation. Certainly, idiomatic expressions fall into* that category. Sometimes, however, translations just won't work because, even though the meaning is clear, the word form is faulty. Sophisticated users of English are delighted with the language's flexibility as verbs become nouns; nouns become adjectives; and adjectives, in turn, become nouns or verbs or adverbs—but not always. Some follow predictable patterns as they change form; others do not and are not easily translated. Not every English word is so elastic.* Consider the following examples of incorrect transformation and missed translation:

1. Missed Translation—The wrong adjective form

Incorrect:
The firm's *absent* compliance with these terms put the deal at risk.

Correct Uses of Absent/Absence:
- Six members of the branch office staff were *absent*.
- In their *absence*, we met.
- The *absent* staff members will receive minutes.
- Absent clear direction, we will use our own guidelines.

Correct Expression of Writer's Intent:
1. The firm's *noncompliance* with these terms put the deal at risk.
2. In the *absence* of compliance, the deal is at risk.
3. *Without compliance*, the deal is at risk.
4. *Lack of* compliance with these terms puts the deal at risk.
5. *Unless the firm complies* with these terms, the deal will be at risk.

---

fall into—to become part of an existing group
elastic—stretchable, flexible

2. Missed Translation—Trying to form a noun by incorrectly adding "icity" to an adjective

Incorrect:
Each candidate must show a high level of *technicity*.

Correct Expression of Writer's Intent:
Each candidate must show a high level of *technical skill*.

A few words do form nouns with *-icity* endings; most are adjectives with a form similar to *technique*.

adjective	noun
ethnic	ethnicity
eccentric	eccentricity
electric	electricity

Technique is the noun form (borrowed from French); *technical* is the English-styled adjective that cannot be made into the noun form with a *-city* ending. There is no way to predict these irregulars. Noun forms should be checked in the dictionary.

3. Missed Translation—Incorrectly creating a verb from a noun

Incorrect:
Sam took a course in hotel management and *restaurantation*.
Correct:
Sam took a course in hotel and *restaurant management*.

Again, check your dictionary. Many words do form nouns with -tion or -sion endings. Most are verbs.

verb	noun
to fascinate	fascination
to exhaust	exhaustion
to confuse	confusion

Restaurant is a noun and can become another noun, *restauranteur*, *one who manages a restaurant* (from the French), but there is no corresponding verb. One *manages* a restaurant.

4. Missed Translation—The wrong part of speech

<u>Incorrect</u>:
I am *exciting* to attend the international seminar.
(*Exciting* is an adjective that describes a noun.)

<u>Correct</u>:
• The international seminar will be *exciting*.
• I am *excited* about attending.

The keynote speaker may be *exciting*, but, the person attending is *excited* about attending. *Excited* describes how the writer, speaker, or attendee feels. It follows a form of the verb to be that links the person with the feeling.

A related problem is illustrated by the translated sentence: *I am boring* by this seminar. Not so: the seminar *is boring*; the attendee (person attending) is *bored*.

5. Missed Translation—Using a noun instead of an adjective

<u>Incorrect</u>:
A *slightly difference* price defeated the competition.
(*Difference* is a noun, not an adjective.)

<u>Correct</u>:
• A *slight difference* in price defeated the competition.
• A slight price *difference* defeated the competition.
• A slightly *different* price defeated the competition.
  (*Difference* is the adjective; it describes.)

6. Missed Translation—Selecting the wrong prefix

<u>Incorrect</u>:
The new administration plans to *irregulate* our industry.

While the prefix *ir-* means *not*, it is not correct in this context. The appropriate prefix is *de-* and the correct word is *deregulate*. Learning the correct prefix when more than one applies is on par with* learning to use prepositions and

---

**on par with*—equal to; the same as

idioms correctly. You just have to memorize. Most grammar books list prefixes and their meanings.

Other examples that would cause similar confusion include:

Correct	Incorrect
derail	unrail
unseat	deseat
ungrateful	ingrateful
ingrate	ungrate
irregular	unregular

7. Missed Translation — Using the wrong word

<u>Incorrect</u>:

Mr. Ziegler is a *reputed* businessman.

<u>Correct Use of Reputed</u>:

Bugsy Segal was a *reputed* crime figure.

Reputed implies a *bad reputation*. The correct word to describe Mr. Ziegler is *reputable*, which means of *good reputation, respectable.*

<u>Correct Expression of Writer's Intent:</u>:

Mr. Ziegler is a *reputable* businessman. (He has a positive reputation, resulting from good reports.)

Meaning arises from a common source term. The form of the word changes its meaning from good to bad.

📃 IT'S YOUR TURN

EXERCISE 1

To become comfortable with transforming words into new parts of speech, fill in the blanks on this chart of word transformations. *You may need a dictionary to find the appropriate noun form.*

Verb (infinitive form)	Present Participle	Past Participle	Noun
to exhaust	exhausting	exhausted	exhaustion
		excited	
to interest			interest
		confused	
to puzzle			
	disappointing		
		terrified	
		fascinated	fascination
to disgust			
to assess	assessing		
			annoyance
to vacation			vacation

Use the blank chart on page 147 to collect your own "transforming" verbs.

Verb (infinitive form)	Present Participle	Past Participle	Noun

PARTICIPLES

The present participles you formed in the second column lead a double life.* They are used for continuous tense verbs *and* they can be used as adjectives to modify other words in the sentence.

VERB
Our team *is reporting* on the airport construction.

ADJECTIVE
Michelle Sontag, the *reporting* officer, filed a complaint.

VERB
The vendor *is requesting* a copy of the print requisition.

ADJECTIVE
The *requesting* agency submitted a proposal last year.

---

double life—to have two distinctly different lives—In espionage, a *double agent*, who leads a *double life*, is a spy for both sides.

Write two sentences, one using the *-ing form of the word interest (interesting)* as a verb, and one using it as an adjective:

_____

_____

The past participles you formed in the third column *also* lead a double life. They are used either as perfect tense verbs (present, past, and future) or as adjectives.

VERB
Mr. Tanaka *has requested* your assistance.

ADJECTIVE
Your *requested* assistance is critical.

Now write two more sentences, one using the past participle of *puzzle* as a verb, and one using it as an adjective.

_____

_____

Present and past participles can also introduce adjective phrases, groups of words that modify as a group.

Finishing [present participle] *the report*, Ling Ling incorporated the new third-quarter figures.

The buyer's bid, **believed** [past participle] *to be his final offer*, is too low.

The experiment design, ***including*** [present participle] *Merrill's formula*, was accepted as proposed.

This herbal remedy **taken** [past participle] *at the onset of a virus* seems to shorten healing time. (*Taken* is the past participle form of the irregular verb *to take*.)

Write a present participle phrase in a sentence.

_____

Write a past participle phrase in a sentence.

_____

NOUN MISFITS *

Sometimes translations don't work because you've pushed the word form into a use where it just doesn't fit. That happens most often when the word you are using can change its part of speech—its grammatical use—in a sentence (as can present and past participles) with no change in form or spelling. Noun misfits* that fit into this category include gerunds, infinitive phrases used as nouns, and noun phrases. English as a second language writers often use these forms interchangeably.

GERUNDS

Let's consider gerunds first. **Gerunds are –ing verb forms used as nouns.** The name doesn't matter, but *understanding the use* does. (In that last sentence, *understanding the use* is a gerund phrase because *understanding* is used as a noun, the subject of the verb *does*.)

Initial confusion in using a gerund form may result from the shift that the –ing verb form takes from verb to noun use. Gerunds are based on verbs and, therefore, indicate action or state of being.

The difference between a verb and a gerund is that a gerund acts, in the sentence, as a noun. It may be used in any placement a noun would be used, for example: as a subject, direct object, subject complement, or object of a preposition.

You will find examples of gerunds and gerund phrases in each of the four above-mentioned sentence positions on the following page. In each example, the gerund is in italics.

Note: Some words can be used as gerunds, some should not be, and some fit only in very specific sentence structures.

---

misfits—things or people that don't fit into a particular situation or group

Gerund as subject:

- *Reading* can be very relaxing.
- *Requesting an application* is the first step.
- *Being* in charge gave Suzanne renewed confidence.

Gerund as direct object:

- My friends love my *cooking*.
- The company recommends *sending* vacation requests early.
- I enjoy *creating* new web designs.

Gerund as subject complement:

- My boss's favorite activity is *complaining*.
- My son's first job was *delivering* papers.
- Sandra's greatest pride has been *creating* order in our office.

Gerund as the object of a preposition:

- You can only improve a skill by *practicing*.
- You will not resolve the problem by *shouting* at each other.
- Paulo received bonus for *bringing* in the most accounts.

INFINITIVES

The infinitive, like the gerund, can also be used as a noun. In the following sentences, the infinitive is used as the subject.

> *To simplify* Martin's report would be a disservice.
> (*To simplify* is the subject of the above sentence.)
> *To speak* during the lecture is rude.
> *To err* is human; *to forgive* is divine.

The infinitive form of the verb (to + the base form), is used in several ways. Sentence structure is one important clue in determining whether you should use an infinitive form; sentence meaning is the other.

The most common placement of infinitives are—

after an adjective: Herman *is ready* **to report**.
after another verb: Herman *is waiting* **to report**.

If an infinitive follows a verb in a negative sentence, the negative follows the initial verb.

Examples: Herman *is* **not** *studying* both systems.
           Herman *agreed* **not** *to send* the report before our department approves it.

INFINITIVES OF PURPOSE

Certain verbs usually take an infinitive (to + simple verb form) as an object: *They intend* **to finance** *that project*. Such infinitives show purpose, the action that the subject of the sentence is taking, did take, or plans to take. (*They* are the persons who are intending *to finance*.)

agree	He *agreed* **to accept** the bid.
appear	The firm *appears* **to be** solvent.
attempt	Don't *attempt* **to negotiate** with them.
be able	*Are* your trainers *able* **to teach** that course?
consent	I *consented* **to lead** the team.
decide	The team leader *will decide* when **to add** staff.
fail	The vendor *failed* **to deliver** on time.
forget	Please don't *forget* **to schedule** the meeting.
hope	We *hope* **to land** that contract.
knows (how)	Pam *knows* how **to get** things done.
understands (how)	Martin *understands how* **to close** a sale.

If, in a sentence, you can replace *to* with *in order to*, the sentence is an **infinitive of purpose**.

Walter is studying both systems (*in order to*) report compatibility problems.

He accepted the bid (*in order to*) move the project along.

Susan agreed with Tom (*in order to*) end the argument.

🖥 IT'S YOUR TURN

EXERCISE 2

Write your own sentences, using the verbs below plus a different verb as an infinitive of purpose.

1. neglect _____

_____

2. offer _____

_____

3. plan _____

_____

4. wants _____

_____

5. refuse _____

_____

6. seem _____

_____

MORE INFINITIVES OF PURPOSE

In each of the sentences in the first section of this chapter, the infinitive of purpose is related to the subject. Some infinitives of purpose, however, are related to an object of the verb.

Examples:

The attorney **advised us to accept** their offer.

(*Attorney* is the subject of the verb *advised*, *us* is the object; *us* refers to the persons whose purpose is to accept.)

allow   The contract *allows* **us** *to open* a second office.

cause   Was it the update that *caused* the **system** *to develop* problems?

convince   His proposal *will convince* the appropriations **committee** *to increase* our budget.

encourage   Good managers *encourage* staff *to help* one another.

want   I *want* my assistant *to get* organized.

IT'S YOUR TURN

EXERCISE 3

Below you will find ten verbs that take an object related to an infinitive of purpose. Write a sentence that includes an infinitive of purpose for each one. The first three are done for you.

1. force   Those contract terms force **us** *to comply* by July 1.

2. invite   Invite the **participants** *to evaluate* the course.

3. order   Your project manager ordered the **engineer** *to submit* revisions immediately.

4. permit _____

   _____

5. persuade _____

   _____

6. remind _____

   _____

7. require _____

   _____

8. teach _____

   _____

9. tell _____

_____

10. urge _____

_____

That-Clauses

A final noun form that's difficult to find when you're reaching for precise translation is in a *that*-clause. *That*-clauses begin with the word *that* and contain a subject and a verb (that he request, that she report). **Caution:** The *that* that begins a noun clause should not be omitted from a sentence in the way you can omit *that* when it begins an adjective clause.

That-clause as adjective:

The budget *that he submitted yesterday* was approved today.

Many writers would omit *that* from the above sentence, and they would be grammatically correct. (The budget *he submitted yesterday* was approved today.) If the clause is used to modify (*that he submitted yesterday* describes—modifies—the word *budget*), the sentence is correct with or without *that*.

The business *that* my brother bought is thriving. *or*
The business my brother bought is thriving.

That-clause as noun:

1. That we proceed with the design seems critical.
2. Her first instruction was that we proceed with the design.

In these sentences, the *that-clause* is used as a noun: as the subject in sentence 1, and as the object in sentence 2. In these sentences, *that* cannot be omitted. This use is sometimes referred to as *conditional* because the noun clause sets up a condition.

As discussed in the Subjunctives section in Chapter 6 (page 135): translation to a noun clause is especially tricky if the noun clause has a third person singular subject (she, he, it, the department, the manager, the applicant, etc.). The usual subject/verb agreement rules don't apply. <u>Third person singular subjects in a noun clause of "condition" take the simple base form of the verb</u> instead of using usual third person singular form with an *s* ending.

Examples:

Regulations required *that* **he** *leave* before April. (not *leaves*)

That the applicant *have* an equal chance made rescheduling necessary. (not *has*)

Her first instruction is *that* he *proceed* with the design. (not *proceeds*)

The chart below summarizes these three ways to use verbs as nouns.

infinitive	gerund (-ing verb as noun)	noun clause
to request	requesting	that he request

infinitive: *To request* all changes in writing is important.
gerund: *Requesting* changes in writing is important.
noun clause: He insists *that you request* changes in writing.

IT'S YOUR TURN

EXERCISE 4

Correct the underlined portion of each sentence, using a gerund, an infinitive phrase, or a that-clause.

1. We have requested <u>the client to get a letter of agreement</u>.

2. <u>They hope to be continuing</u> their relationship in the future.

3. <u>He explained that to review the report</u> is a requirement.

4. The figures show <u>the company to commit to a new policy</u>.

5. The new manager anticipates <u>to incur substantial expenses.</u>

6. <u>To be vacationing in Europe</u> may require a lot of planning.

7. I objected <u>to remove computer training</u> from the budget.

8. <u>To delay final approval</u> is a strategy they have used before.

IT'S YOUR TURN

EXERCISE 5

Edit the following paragraph, changing words and phrases that didn't translate grammatically. Problems are underlined; there are many possible editing solutions.

RE: Manufacture and export of trailer

<u>Forwarding</u> of our phone conversation on July 5, 2006, I attach requirements of <u>constructions to construct</u> the trailer. <u>To be meeting</u> all US safety <u>guidances</u> is a <u>reputed</u> strength of our company. For more than 20 years, our company <u>that is experienced</u> in all segments of the <u>manufacturizing</u> has also exported to US customers. Our regulations <u>require to fill out</u> the form you will <u>find out</u> in the <u>attachment</u> papers. <u>To complete this form</u> is necessary <u>that we begin manufacture of</u> the trailer. We <u>understanding</u> you <u>are asking our company supply</u> the entire trailer to you.

NOUNS THAT NEVER CHANGE

The last section discussed some of the more complicated noun uses in the language. This section continues examining noun problems. In this case, however, misuse occurs because the noun form remains surprisingly simple: it doesn't even change form in the plural.

Most nouns in English form the plural by adding "s." (Many irregular nouns change form in other ways when plural.) Some remain the same for singular and plural uses.

We have already introduced the concept of count and non-count nouns in Chapter 3, as this distinction affects article usage. This section offers more details, examples, and practice, but you might want to review the introduction and exercises beginning on page 45.

The nouns listed below do not form plurals by adding "s." They are known as "non-count nouns."

aircraft	livestock	consensus	punctuation
credit	research	deer	sheep
foodstuff	trout	information	machinery
stationery	laughter	helium	furniture

Context also affects usage. In the following sentences, the singular or plural form of the noun is determined by the noun's use in the sentence:

Varying *amounts* of solvent affect the formula.
The *amount* of risk is significant.
The water *level* is high.
The *level* of risk is great.
Several *levels* of management exist.
The *total* cost of the renovation is exorbitant.
The *totals* of each column are used as marketing tools.

IT'S YOUR TURN

EXERCISE 6

Correct the singular/plural noun usage in these sentences.

1. The overall risks is acceptable.
2. The level of risks is too high.
3. Kim approved the company's credits with our bank.
4. The account payables were up last quarter.
5. The agency received many letter of credits.
6. Send the letters of credits to the bank.
7. PAK is one of the top company in Asia.

Don't be afraid to explore noun uses in translation. Dictionaries give good guidance for noun and adjective forms, and upper-level grammar books give more practice in using noun clauses, gerunds, and infinitive phrases.

ANSWER KEY

EXERCISE I

Verb (infinitive form)	Present Participle	Past Participle	Noun
to exhaust	exhausted	exhausted	exhaustion
to excite	exciting	excited	excitement
to interest	interesting	interested	interest
to confuse	confusing	confused	confusion
to puzzle	puzzling	puzzled	puzzlement
to disappoint	disappointing	disappointed	disappointment
to terrify	terrifying	terrified	terror
to fascinate	fascinating	fascinated	fascination
to disgust	disgusting	disgusted	disgust
to assess	assessing	assessed	assessment
to annoy	annoying	annoyed	annoyance
to vacation	vacationing	vacationed	vacation

EXERCISE 2 *Possible answers:*

Suggested sentences using subject-related infinitives with the verbs listed:

1. Chances are he *will neglect **to mail*** a follow-up report.

2. Mr. Habib *offered **to review*** the proposal.

3. Do you *plan **to join*** the association?

4. Kira *wants **to be*** a writer.

5. Ms. Russell *refuses **to see*** him.

6. We *seem **to lose*** money every month.

EXERCISE 3 *Possible answers:*

4. The new regulations do not permit employees to use instant messaging.

5. Bill was finally persuaded to buy a digital camera.

6. My pop-up calendar reminded me to call the office.

7. OSHA requires all employers to use this form.

8. My grandson taught me how to build a website.

9. Before you leave, tell Beth to lock up.

10. Doctors urge their patients to get regular exercise.

EXERCISE 4

1. We have requested *that the client get a letter of agreement.*

2. *They hope to continue* their relationship in the future.

3. He explained *that reviewing the report* is a requirement.

4. The figures show *that the company is committed to a new policy.*   *or*

   The figures show *that the company should commit to a new policy.*

5. The auditor anticipates *incurring substantial expenses* during third quarter.

6. *Answering the phone* throughout the registration period may require a second receptionist.

7. I objected to *removing computer training* from the budget.

8. *Delaying final approval* is a strategy they have used before.

EXERCISE 5 *Suggested Answers:*

RE: Manufacture and export of trailer

<u>As I promised</u> in our phone conversation on July 5, 2006, I attach <u>construction requirements</u> for the trailer. <u>Meeting</u> all US safety <u>guidelines</u> is a <u>strength</u> of our company. (*or,* Our company has a <u>good reputation</u> for meeting all US safety guidelines.) For more than 20 years, our company, <u>experienced</u> in all segments of manufacturing, has also exported to US customers. Our regulations require that <u>you fill out the attached form</u>. (*or,* Our regulations require <u>you to fill out the attached form</u>.) <u>Completing this form</u> is necessary before we can begin manufacturing the trailer. (*or,* <u>Completion</u> of this form is necessary <u>before manufacturing can begin</u>.) We <u>understand that you are asking our company to supply</u> the entire trailer to you. (*or,* We understand that you are asking that our <u>company supply</u> the entire trailer to you.)

EXERCISE 6

1. The overall risk is acceptable. *or*
   The overall risks are acceptable.
2. The level of risk is too high.
3. Kim approved the company's credit with our bank.
4. The accounts payable[1] were up last quarter.
5. The agency received many letters of credit.
6. Send the letters of credit[2] to the bank.
7. PAK is one of the top companies in Asia.

[1,2] *Accounts payable* and *letters of credit* are examples of compound nouns that form plurals with the "primary" or key word in the compound. Other examples are *daughters-in-law* and *passersby.*

The Editing Process

8

- Whose Writing Is It, Anyway?
- Editing for Correct Punctuation
- Editing for Style
- Editing for ESL Errors

WHOSE WRITING IS IT, ANYWAY?

Although most people dread the task of writing, once they have pen in hand or computer keys at their fingertips, they become very possessive—of their words and of their style. Do you sign your own work? Does someone else's name go on it? Do you write as a member of a team? Who has the ultimate responsibility for your report or your research? If that person is someone other than you, you know that you do not have the final word— or the final stroke of the pen or keyboard.

You can make the editing process easier. First, notice consistent changes. Does the person who edits your work regularly change past tense to present, passive voice to active, or pronouns to nouns? If so, you must ask yourself a basic question: *Does the edit improve the writing?* Accepting the edit that improves is easy.

Even if the editing change is just different, not better, it's sometimes best to accept it. Chances are, your editor will make the same kinds of edits regularly. You can discuss those with which you disagree, but as long as that person remains your editor, you can save a lot of time by adopting some of his or her writing techniques.

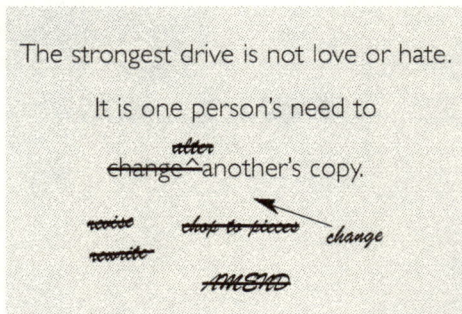

The strongest drive is not love or hate. It is one person's need to ~~change~~ alter another's copy.

The letter on page 165 was edited by a supervisor who likes some "businessese" expressions so much that these expressions have become pet* phrases. The director also prefers concise wording and direct sentences that use simple tense forms.

---

pet—personal favorite

Dear Mr. Sanchez:

Please be advised that
~~I have been speaking to Precise Print about your brochure.~~ T^t~~he~~

at Precise Print
manager ^ ~~there~~ has informed me that 15,000 brochures will be

~~being~~ delivered to the warehouse on Thursday, July 16~~th.~~ This

uses *needs*
piece will be using several custom colors and ~~will be needing~~

more time to dry ~~before sending, and~~ so print time is a week

longer than we thought~~. and that is why delivery is on the~~

~~Thursday.~~ The first several sample pieces will be delivered to

me for approval, probably on Wednesday afternoon. I will ~~be~~

call~~ing~~ you when I get those and you can look at them too.

Please call with any questions: 800-464-9000. Thank you.
Sincerely,

Rita Pearl
Production Manger

After reviewing her supervisor's changes, Rita should be able to write a letter that fits this person's editorial preferences. If she can learn to do that, she will save both herself and her supervisor time.

Look at the two versions of e-mails on page 166, each written by Rita. Which one will her supervisor be most likely to approve without editorial changes?

Version A

Subject: Manuscript Rewrites

Please be advised that the printer needs a final layout by August 4. Since we need two weeks to complete layout before we submit to the client, we must know when you will send us your file. Please call me at 555-222-1986 with your target submission date so we can put you in our schedule. Thank you.

Version B

Subject: Manuscript Rewrites

When I called the printer he said he needed our final by August 4th. Would you please let me know when we can have the final draft of your copy? We will be working on layout for two weeks after we get your copy, and before we will be submitting the layout to the client for approval. So we will need to know a date at which you can send us your copy, and I would appreciate it if you could call me at 464-9000. Thank you very much.

Rita's director would probably choose Version A for the following reasons:

- ✎ It's clear and direct and uses a simple style.

- ✎ It includes the pet phrases the editor feels comfortable with: Please be advised that; please call (with phone number); and the simple thank you conclusion.

- ✎ Version A uses statements rather than questions.

- ✎ The extra phrases in Version B were deleted in Version A, especially those "polite fillers."

Sometimes, your editor doesn't improve your writing. What should you do if the edits are contrary to everything you know about clear, concise writing? First, tread lightly.* Understand that someone's (your editor's) ego is on the line.* Following are suggestions for opening a dialogue on writing style.

GUIDELINES FOR A "COOPERATIVE EDITING" DIALOGUE

1. **Make an appointment.** Advance notice helps both of you prepare for the discussion, even if the preparation is confined to thinking about the editing process.

2. **Base your comments and questions on actual material.** Save copies of all your edited drafts, which you might give to your editor in advance. Remember, the best editorial relationships are cooperative. Make the first move in this cooperative effort by sharing your materials.

3. **Begin the meeting with general discussion questions about writing and about the editor's expectations.**

   ✍ What writing tasks will you be expected to do?

   ✍ What general guidelines (or samples) does the company or department have for these written documents?

   ✍ What specific language and/or ESL issues does the editor see in your present work?

4. **During the meeting, ask specific questions about edits you don't agree with or those you don't understand.**

5. **Discuss specific writing/editing samples.** It's also a good idea to bring a new piece to edit together.

6. **Listen, take notes, and make another appointment to discuss your progress.**

---

tread lightly—to be careful
on the line—at risk, exposed

Always keep in mind your real goals: to keep your job and to do it effectively. If accepting some inflated language or pet phrases will help you achieve those goals, accept them.

All business writers, whether native speakers or foreign-born, must negotiate an effective, cooperative editing relationship in the workplace. Publication, even internal publication, has always been a road to advancement.

EDITING FOR CORRECT PUNCTUATION

As you learn to edit your own work more effectively, you might begin by developing editorial reading habits. One of the simplest of these is reading for punctuation. Editors automatically judge the punctuation and capitalization in the newspapers and magazines they read. So can you. Make it a habit to judge punctuation in published material. Usually it's correct. If you know why it's there, you, too, will be able to punctuate correctly when the same reasons apply in your own writing.

Read the "must-know" example that follows. The reasons for the punctuation marks are in the Punctuation Endnotes after the example. Then try Exercise 1. The example, with its notations, provides a good review of punctuation, but certainly is not the whole story.* Check a good reference book for more punctuation rules. (We recommend *Grammar in Plain English*.)

---

the whole story—everything you need to know; all the facts

Punctuation "Must-Knows"

Read the following article excerpt. Each mark of punctuation is footnoted and explained in the Punctuation Endnotes on pages 170 and 171. (Numbers are repeated when usage reoccurs.)

Cost-effective[1] Print Material

For most small businesses,[2] this season has been characterized by scattered attempts to reach a cautious market through a smaller advertising budget. Smart budgeting, however,[3] requires more than just cutting last year's[4] big-ticket items;[5] it rests on planning. When applied to producing printed sales materials,[2] planning means that you should take the time to maximize a printed piece's[4] value *before*[6] you spend money printing it.

Consider the proposed piece's[4] versatility. A price tag for producing the proposed piece is easier to judge after you've[7] determined its[8] versatility. A piece can be used in several ways:[9] as a handout at trade shows, in a counter display, as a bill stuffer to your current customers, as a direct mail piece to bring in new business,[10] and as a part of a more complete proposal package. One piece can do all this and more—[11] if it's[7] well planned.

Size affects use. The ubiquitous 8 1/2" by 11",[12] three-panel[1] brochure earned its popularity by being the right size. It fits into a standard number 10 business envelope;[5] it works as a direct mailer with one panel as a detachable business reply card;[5] it fits in a jacket pocket when used as a handout;[5] and it mixes well with other pieces in a presentation folder. Whatever size you decide is right for your own intended uses,[2] make sure you can mail the piece in some way (self-mailer,[13] special envelope)[14] and that it can be included with your other business materials.

Content affects versatility. To make sure a piece has "shelf-life,"[13,15] that it can be used for an extended period of time,[16] avoid time-related[1] phrases like "this fall," "by the end of the year," or "2008 prices."[15] Focus copy on the strongest marketing points you can make about your offerings, points that can be trusted to remain true for the period during which you want to use the piece. Consider whether phone numbers or addresses are likely to change;[5] adjust copy accordingly. Maybe it's[7] time to get an 800 number. This might become the one printed piece you don't[7] have to throw away when your company moves![17] Most important,[2] rewrite copy until you're[7] satisfied that you have good attention-getting[1] headlines and clear explanations of your offerings. You'll[7] reuse those elements in letters, ads, premiums, presentations,[9] and proposals.

Design affects versatility. When you look at the initial design,[2] try to imagine some portion of it as a newspaper ad, as a poster, even as a magnet. If the proposed print piece has strong graphics, enough open space to allow easy readability of copy,[10] and a clearly recognizable business name or logo,[2] you're[7] already saving money on future design costs for a whole range of marketing and advertising spin-offs.[13]*

PUNCTUATION ENDNOTES

1. Hyphen—Joins two words that are used as an adjective when they precede a noun.

2. Comma—Follows introductory phrases and dependent clauses.

3. Comma—Sets off words or phrases that interrupt the flow of a sentence and can be omitted without changing the meaning.

---

spin off—a new and distinctly separate product that incorporates major components of an earlier product

4. Apostrophe—Shows possession, even in possessive-styled adjectives (this year's winner; the team's job; the budget's total).

5. Semicolon—Connects two complete, related thoughts that could be separate sentences. Can these thoughts be separated by a period? If so, they can be joined by a semicolon.

6. Italics—Show emphasis.

7. Apostrophe—Replaces the omitted letters in a contraction.

8. NO Apostrophe—Don't use an apostrophe in possessive pronouns, and don't confuse possessive pronouns with contractions.

9. Colon—Introduces a list or announces a key point.

10. Comma—Separates three or more items in a series. Most companies prefer not to use the final serial comma. However, it is preferred in long or complex sentences to add clarity.

11. Dash—Separates—strongly—a phrase from the rest of the sentence.

12. Comma—Separates two adjectives that modify the same noun.

13. Hyphen—Connects two or more words that form a noun

14. Parentheses—Used to insert supporting or explanatory information into the middle of a sentence or paragraph. Place the parenthetical phrase as close as possible to the word it describes.

15. Quotation marks—Identify jargon or unfamiliar terms as well as words directly quoted from some other source. Notice the placement of the comma. Commas and periods always go inside quotation marks.

16. Comma—Separate a phrase that interrupts the flow of the sentence. In this case, a defining phrase is separated by commas.

17. Exclamation mark—Used at the end of a sentence that shows excitement or strong emphasis. Exclamation marks are almost always inappropriate in business writing. Use sparingly and only in informal or promotional writing.

⌨ IT'S YOUR TURN

FROM YOUR FILES 🗁   Select two letters from your files.
Use the above sample to review punctuation rules. Can you
determine the reasons for the punctuation in the two letters?
Don't worry if you can't identify a reason for every punctuation
mark; in fact, you may find errors in punctuation.

EDITING FOR STYLE

When you write a first draft, it's not likely to be concise.
Drafts, as pointed out in Chapter 1, are supposed to be fast, not
perfect. Your first editing pass should be like pruning*. To cut
the excess words and leave only those that are necessary, learn
to employ these three very effective editing techniques.

1. **Use active voice.** (See Chapter 4.)

    Unedited: The customers were kept waiting for an hour.

    Edited: The customers waited for an hour.   *or*
    The cafe kept its customers waiting for an hour.

2. **Limit your use of prepositional phrases.** (See Chapter 4.)

    Unedited: Members of the team of the marketing manager
    met yesterday.

    Edited: The marketing manager's team met yesterday.

3. **Cut unnecessary words and phrases.** (See Chapter 2.)

    Unedited: We are thankful to you for being a speaker at
    our company's highly motivational conference.

    Edited: Thank you for speaking at our conference.

---

pruning—trimming, as pruning bushes

IT'S YOUR TURN

EXERCISE I

Correct the sentences below, editing for style.

Use active voice.

1. The payment was submitted too late.

2. Our new ads were designed by Big Co, Inc.

3. Even after review, the procedures were changed six times.

4. Customer complaints were cited as the primary reason to add new phone operators.

Limit use of prepositional phrases.
(Prepositional phrases are in parentheses).

1. We arranged a meeting (with the manager) (of loans) (in New York).

2. (Over this weekend) the investors (from Indonesia) gathered (at our central office) to learn (about the advantages) (of our new methods) (for marketing).

3. (Of the many requests) (for clarification) (of the proposal guidelines), none (of them) was as compelling (in its nature) (as the demand) (from the CEO) (to shorten) the guidelines (by cutting) (at least) ten pages (of it).

Cut unnecessary words and phrases.

1. There are two possible approaches that we are considering.

2 The potential for future adverse effects that might threaten the success of this experiment is thought to be substantial.

3. The reason for caution is because the client has strong and firm opinions as to how to advertise the item of which we speak.

🖳 IT'S YOUR TURN

EXERCISE 2

Prune excess words: (1) Passive sentences are marked by (P).
Change as many as possible to active voice. (2) Shorten or
delete at least some phrases in parentheses. (3) Reread, cutting
other unnecessary words. **Hint:** Cutting *there is, there are,* and
there were often improves style. **Hint 2:** Delete "extra" modifiers that do not add new information.

DATABASE REPORT

PURPOSE: To update the current system being used for
Connect clients, agencies, and statistical data reports using
Paradox.

PROCEDURE: (P) There <u>were</u> three databases <u>created</u>
through the manipulation of tables, reports, forms, and queries
in Paradox. (The three are as follows): an individual Connect
client database that contains (information related to the
Connect program), secondly, an aggregate database (that takes
numerical data into account), and lastly an agency database
that provides information (about various health care facilities)
(in Central Harlem.)

CONNECT CLIENT DATABASE: (P) The Connect client
database <u>was created</u> (to allow) (for easy access) (of individual Connect clients.) (P) (It was created) (with several tables)
(in Paradox.) (P) The original fields <u>were taken</u> (from a previous program) (in DataEase); however, there *were* a number
(of additional fields) *added* (to maximize usage) (of the existing tables). It contains (information as to) the person's name,
address, telephone number, enrollment status, (date of birth),
ethnicity, recertification date, s.s.#, case management team,
and Medicaid status. (There *is* also information *stored* as to)
the client's specific risk factors, means of support, and, lastly,
any services (either needed or received) (by the client.)

EDITING FOR ESL ERRORS

So far, this chapter has concentrated on editing skills that any writer can use to polish his or her own work. The next exercise contains trouble spots specific to ESL writers.

IT'S YOUR TURN

EXERCISE 3

Edit the letter below. There are many correct ways to rewrite.

Dear Mrs. Ramires:

I apologize the delay of this message, but I am pleased giving you following information on our Alpaca Sweaters manufactured by our factory using 100 percent alpaca wool.

Enclosed brochure will give you an idea of the variety of sweater that you may considering for buying, as we are sending to you samples of what could be of your interest.

Most of our clients in California are pleased with our quality and you will enjoy samples that you may sell as hot bread* and be sure that our company will be delighted doing business with you.

Sincerely,
Georgi Kristos

---

*sell like hotcakes (not like hot bread)—describing a popular item that sells quickly; in the idiom, like is used instead of the grammatically correct as.

SUMMARY

Editing is a circular process. You edit, rewrite, edit, rewrite until you're satisfied. Then you send your writing to another person, who does the same thing. You may receive others' written work and become their editor. Whenever you edit, read several times: once for the logic and clarity of the writing, once for grammar, once for typos and spelling, and once for tone and style. Don't try to edit everything during the same reading. Start with the Editor's and ESL Checklists in Chapter 1, and develop your own personal list of items to look for as you edit.

EXERCISE I

Active Voice

1. Patti submitted the payment too late.

2. Big Co, Inc. designed our new ads.

3. Even after review, the committee changed the procedures six times.

   or The committee changed the procedures six times after review.

4. The consultant cited customer complaints as the primary reason to add new phone operators.

Passive Phrases

1. We arranged a meeting with the New York loan manager.

2. (Last weekend), the Indonesian investors gathered (at our central office)* to learn the advantages of our new marketing methods.

   *(Note: Place may be unimportant; if so, delete this phrase from formal business writing.)

3. None of the many requests for clarification was as compelling as the CEO's demand that we cut ten pages of the proposal's guidelines.

Unnecessary Words and Phrases

1. We are considering two approaches.

2. Future adverse effects may threaten the success of this experiment.

3. Be careful; the client has strong opinions about how to advertise this item.

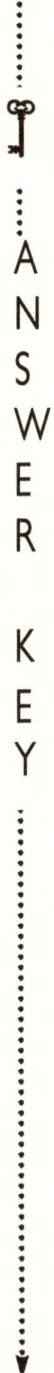

EXERCISE 2

DATABASE REPORT

PURPOSE: To use Paradox to update the system currently used for Connect clients, agencies, and statistical data reports.

PROCEDURE: The project team manipulated tables, reports, forms, and queries in Paradox to create three databases: an individual Connect client database (that contains) (or containing) Connect program information; an aggregate database for numerical data, and an agency database (that) provides (or providing) information about Central Harlem health care facilities.

CONNECT CLIENT DATABASE: The Connect client database allows easy access to individual client information/data through several tables in Paradox. The team used the original fields from a previous program in DataEase; however, they added a number of fields to enhance those tables. The database contains the client's name, address, telephone number, enrollment status, birth date, ethnicity, recertification date, s.s.#, case management team, and Medicaid status. Also stored are client's specific risk factors, means of support, and services the client either needed or received.

EXERCISE 3

Dear Mrs. Ramires:

I apologize for the delay of this message, but I am pleased to give you the following information about our alpaca sweaters, made from 100 percent alpaca wool.

The enclosed brochure will give you an idea of the variety of sweaters that you may consider. We are sending samples of what could (or may) interest you.

Most of our clients in California are pleased with our quality, and we are sure that you will enjoy these samples, which should sell like hotcakes. Our company will be delighted to do business with you.

Sincerely,

Giorgi Kristos

9

Form and Format

American businesses are constantly trying to create uniform documents that simplify both writing and reading. Documents that follow predictable, logical formats simplify both processes. The writer is familiar with form and structure; the reader is better able to skim and, in a long document, knows where to find specific content.

If your company is using a uniform format for reports, proposals, or routine correspondence, your writing task is easier. If you are creating your own structure and format, this chapter gives some practical advice. Investigate. Ask to see copies of reports, proposals, letters, and memos written in a style of which your company approves.

FOCUSED DOCUMENTS

Whether you are writing a report, a proposal, or an employee evaluation, you want to keep your document focused. Many of the techniques that help you focus and move the reader through a document are appropriate to any business writing project; most techniques are simple to use.

STRONG PARAGRAPHS

A strong business paragraph begins with the main point (topic sentence) and continues with supporting details. Topic sentences can occur any place in a paragraph in other forms of writing, but for a strong business style, lead with the main point. Save more creative paragraph writing for novels or personal letters.

Once you state your purpose or your recommendation, support it with clear, concise, concrete facts. Keep each paragraph short (five or six sentences) and focused on one topic.

Here is an example of a strong paragraph:

Company A purchases heavy machinery from manufacturers through the Acquisitions Department. The Acquisitions Department is responsible for drafting contracts (to determine the number of machines to be acquired, settlement dates, and servicing fees) between the company and the manufacturer. Once a contract is agreed upon, the Equipment Department is responsible for maintaining the machinery.

Notice that this paragraph is not a series of simple, repetitive statements. You, too, will want to vary your sentence structure and select the most effective ways to combine your ideas.

TRANSITIONS

Transition words build bridges between your ideas and allow the reader to travel easily from topic to topic. They can link sentences within a paragraph, or they can link paragraphs or sections within a longer document. Some commonly-used transition words and their functions are listed below.

Indicate place:	near, nearby, here, where, wherever, next to, adjacent to
Indicate time:	now, then, meanwhile, later, before, after, since
Show sequence:	next, first, second, last
Emphasize:	indeed, in fact, certainly, clearly, of course, naturally
Change gears*:	yet, however, but, although, nonetheless, on the contrary, in contrast, on the other hand, nevertheless
Compare:	similarly, just as, as though
Illustrate:	for example, for instance, to illustrate

---

change gears—automotive reference; to shift or change emphasis

Show cause and effect: consequently, because, therefore, as a result, if/then

Wrap up*: therefore, in conclusion, in summary, finally, in other words

Add: moreover, in addition, too, also, besides, additionally

IT'S YOUR TURN

EXERCISE 1

Select the correct transition words from the previous list to complete the paragraphs. Notice how the correct transition helps you move through the passage.

The Free World Marketplace has increased security substantially _____the recent threats. _____ the tight security process slows visitors, most employees are grateful for the cautious approach. _____, security personnel have noticed that FWM visitors also welcome the concern for safety.

There are, _____ always those who will find fault. _____, a small corp of FWM tenants regularly complains about the inconvenience.

KEY WORDS

When you repeat key words in your writing, you create natural transitions from sentence to sentence and from paragraph to paragraph. Key words can be nouns or verbs that announce your main points (or synonyms for those nouns and verbs), or they can be words that continue central themes within your discussion (a progression through time, a step-by-step manufacturing process, a place-by-place geographic description).

---

*wrap up—to bring to a conclusion

The following paragraph illustrates key word transitioning:

> Metro Corporation began in **2001** with a **4,000** square foot building and a production staff of **eight**. During the **past two years**, Metro Corporation has expanded to occupy an **8,000** square foot building and to employ a production staff of **twenty-three**. Since its expansion, Metro Corporation's gross sales have **doubled** each year.

Three patterns drive the paragraph: passage of time, size of workspace, and number of employees.

IT'S YOUR TURN

EXERCISE 2

Find the words that act as "natural transition" words. Circle them. Are they time-related, process-related, or location related? Do numbers drive you through the paragraph?

1. In 2003, the Clever Corporation produced 4 billion widgets, which accounted for 65 percent of the US market. In addition, Clever sold gotwids, which it imported from a Chinese supplier (Ying, Inc.). The sale of the Chinese imports gave Clever another 8 percent of its domestic market. At year-end 2005, the corporation had increased its production capability to 5 billion and had decreased its imports. Consequently, by the end of 2005, Clever controlled 75 percent of the US market.

2. Perfectly Lovely, Inc. owns five integrated manufacturing facilities that produce fiberboard. Two of the five production plants are in North Carolina: in Raleigh and in Greensboro, the company headquarters. The Raleigh facility is currently under renovation, and Lovely expects it to be back in full production by September 2007. Lovely's largest facility, in Red Hook, Texas, was able to meet the production shortages caused by the Raleigh renovation. Red Hook was also able to maintain its average production

volume per year, while increasing its production to meet the Raleigh shortfall.

Making integration complete, Lovely's remaining two facilities support the company's primary production lines by processing raw materials, in the Cleveland, Ohio, foundry, and by manufacturing molds and dies for Cleveland at the Erie, Pennsylvania, facility.

STRINGING PARAGRAPHS TOGETHER

Group all paragraphs that deal with closely related topics or with an expanded development of the same topic.

Arrange paragraphs within each group in logical progression.

Clear, strong writing may progress:
through **time**
through a **causal process**
through **geographic space**
or through **action**, step by step

Persuasive writing may progress:
from the **known to** the **new** (or the *news*)
from the **basic to** the **complex**
from the **current to** the **proposed or projected**
or from the **general** to the **specific**
(A general statement introduces specific examples.)

SUBHEADINGS

Headings announce the beginning of an important discussion, and subheadings assure the reader that he or she is not lost, but is exploring the issue more thoroughly. Subheadings also help you, the writer, focus your document and avoid repetition.

🖳 IT'S YOUR TURN

EXERCISE 3

Read the Conference Report that follows. Select appropriate paragraph breaks and create and insert helpful subheadings.

Regional Infrastructure Conference

On Thursday, April 7, I attended the Regional Infrastructure Conference in Atlanta, which attracted a wide variety of government officials, professionals, and municipal goods and service providers. There was even a representative from the State Senate. The conference covered a number of topics, from an environmental panel to discussions on new technology. One panel included representatives from the shipping industry and the program included a tour of the Port of Atlanta. On the down side, only municipalities that can offer the necessary services through cooperative efforts will be the winners in the long run. It is apparent that neither state nor local budgets can cover the increasing costs of municipal services. The main theme throughout the conference was the need for long-range planning and shared services over the next decade. During the next several months, conference attendees will meet in small focus groups to address concerns raised. The results of these focus groups will serve as the basis for a Regional Long-Range Plan. Those interested in participating should call Frank Baran, Planning Coordinator.

WHITE SPACE

Headings, subheads, lists, summary tables, and indented paragraphs all create "white space." Don't be afraid to leave white space; readers appreciate it. When you place a heading or subheading on a line surrounded by space, the reader is able to skim the document, assessing its content. It also helps you highlight information you want to emphasize by leading the reader's eye—and attention—to important points.

Look at this example from *Enterprising Women* Magazine (Vol. 6, No. 4, 2005).

Fear-Less Motivation

by Harriet Diamond
& Linda Eve Diamond

Employers, from CEOs to managers, can choose to motivate through policies and responses that show they care. Fear-based motivation (also called *or else*-style motivation), is still popular on reality shows. However, this method now proves to be less effective than more respectful motivational styles.

The new model of a productive work-place is positive, communicative, and respectful. It's the fear-less model: The employee does not walk on eggshells, fearing an environment that stifles creativity and initiative; the employer does not fear losing respect for being "too soft" when being caring and supportive.

Fear-less motivations still sets boundaries, of course, but it is more about being flexible and tapping into what people have to offer; it is not about being rigid and tapping into fear.

Motivating Factor #1:
A Positive Environment

"Nothing great was ever achieved without enthusiasm," Ralph Waldo Emerson said in 1885. That statement is still true today.

Positive vibes are contagious, as are negative ones, so keep your attitude healthy. A negative employer can infect even the most positive people. The "dis-ease" of negativism can spread all the way to your clients or customers.

Positive feedback helps the "so-so" employee become good, the good employee become even better, and the better employee become outstanding.

Remember, a customer is far more likely to have a bad experience with an employee who feels mistreated or "dumped upon" than with an employee who feels competent and appreciated. In treating your employee the way you would have them treat your customers, you are modeling the behavior you expect to see from them.

In a positive work environment, everyone is valued, and no one is "just a (receptionist, clerk, low-level manager, custodian...)." Employers and employees alike know that everyone at the company can make a contribution and every contribution matters. In a positive work environment, no one is dehumanized—everyone rates eye contact and/or a friendly greeting from others at the company.

Motivating Factor #2:
Feedback

Positive Feedback helps the "so-so" employee become good, the good employee become even better, and the better employee become outstanding.

In the early 1980s, one business school instructor was known for introducing the acronym, KTA—the figurative kick in the butt—as the motivational cure-all. Today, the pat on the back goes much farther.

Developmental feedback—the act of sharing with employees what they are doing wrong, why it is wrong, and how they can correct it—

🖥 IT'S YOUR TURN

EXERCISE 4

Look at the thumbnail* page layouts below. This visualizing technique is used by mechanical artists to assess the balance of a page. It also is an easy way to judge whether key points are "skimmable." Place X's on each page where the text draws the eye (and attention).

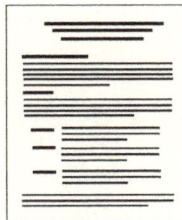

---

*thumbnail—a small presentation of a larger graphic or page (helpful in design and layout)

SPECIFIC FORMATS

Most companies have a prescribed format for job descriptions and performance appraisals. Problems occur when specific formats do not exist. Often, those writing monthly reports and meeting minutes have the freedom to follow their muse.* This freedom adds to the anxiety that may accompany a writing task. Knowing where and how to arrange information simplifies the task considerably.

Following are suggestions for several types of reports. They are only one approach. The Internal Report Worksheet should assist in helping you focus your document.

THE MONTHLY REPORT

Time Period:	The period covered by the report
Purpose:	What the report should accomplish
Key Issues:	The key, relevant issues that surfaced during the report period
Actions Taken:	Actions taken, time periods, and the reason for the actions during the report period
Actions Scheduled:	Key, relevant actions scheduled, time periods, and reasons
Requests or Recommendations:	Your requests or recommendations based on the information in the report

---

muse—source of creative inspiration

An Internal Report Worksheet, like the one that follows, will help you identify key content and format issues. By focusing on your "readers" (audience) and the document's "uses" (purpose) you get your jump start. Clearly stating "the most difficult aspects," you know what problems you must address. By determining "format requirements" and "usual length," you have an idea of structure. By reviewing "the most frequent editorial comments" you have received, you can address them in your role as first editor.

Internal Report Worksheet

Department _____

Document _____

1. The readers of this document:

2. The uses of this document:

3. The most difficult aspect in preparing and/or writing this document:

4. Format requirements:

5. Usual length:

Most frequent editorial comments:

REPORT WRITING STRUCTURE

Executive summary:
Includes conclusions or recommendations if any were reached. Be brief; usually one paragraph is sufficient.

Background:
Positions the report in the larger scheme of things:

- relevance to specific projects already underway or proposed

- relevance to corporate objectives

- relevance to present budget

"Background" also explains how the report was researched, *if that isn't already known to the reader.*

Findings:
Organized by topic classifications. Arranged to emphasize most important points (main points up front).

Analysis:
In a short report, analysis includes findings. If the report is long enough to justify a separate conclusions section, analysis includes final recommendations.

Conclusions:
Stated in direct, clear, positive language. This is another summary paragraph; it's necessary; readers appreciate closure.

EXERCISE 1

Answers may vary, but these choices are the clearest.

The Free World Marketplace has increased security substantially **since** the recent threats. **Although** the tight security process slows visitors, most employees are grateful for the cautious approach. **In addition/Moreover/ Similarly**, security personnel have noticed that FWM visitors also welcome the concern for safety.

There are, **however**, always those who will find fault. **For example/For instance**, a small corps of FWM tenants regularly complains about the inconvenience.

EXERCISE 2

("Natural transition words" are shown here in italics.)

1. *In 2003*, Clever Corporation produced 4 billion widgets, which accounted for *65 percent* of the US market. *In addition,* Clever sold gotwids, which it imported from a Chinese supplier (Ying, Inc.). The sale of the Chinese imports gave Clever another *8 percent* of its domestic market. *At year-end* 2005, the corporation had increased its production capability to 5 billion, and decreased its imports. *Consequently*, by the end of 2005, Clever controlled *75 percent* of the U.S. market.

(In addition and *consequently* are classic transition words.)

2. Perfectly Lovely, Inc. owns *five* integrated manufacturing facilities that produce fiberboard. *Two of the five* production plants are in North Carolina: in Raleigh and in Greensboro, the company headquarters. The Raleigh facility is currently under renovation and Lovely expects it to be back in full production by September 2007. *Lovely's largest facility*, in Red Hook, Texas, was able to meet the production short-

ages caused by the Raleigh renovation. Red Hook was also able to maintain its average production volume per year, while increasing its production to meet the Raleigh shortfall.

Making integration complete, Lovely's *remaining two* facilities support the company's primary *production* lines by *processing* raw materials, in the Cleveland, Ohio foundry, and by *manufacturing* molds and dies for Cleveland at the Erie, Pennsylvania facility.

(*Produce* and *production* also become key words through their repetition; the reader begins to "key into" the information concerning production.)

EXERCISE 3

Regional Infrastructure Conference

Broad-based Participation
On Thursday, April 7, I attended the Regional Infrastructure Conference in Atlanta, which attracted a wide variety of government officials, professionals, and municipal goods and service providers. There was even a representative from the State Senate.

The conference covered a number of topics, from an environmental panel to discussions on new technology. One panel included representatives from the shipping industry, and the program included a tour of the Port of Atlanta.

Implementation Problems
On the down side, only municipalities that can offer the necessary services through cooperative efforts will be the winners in the long run. It is apparent that neither state nor local budgets can cover the increasing costs of municipal services.

Conference Theme

The main theme throughout the conference was the need for long-range planning and shared services over the next decade.

Follow-up

During the next several months, conference attendees will meet in small focus groups to address concerns raised. The results of these focus groups will serve as the basis for a Regional Long-Range Plan. Those interested in participating should call Frank Baran, Planning Coordinator.

EXERCISE 4

Notice that your X's would show attention drawn to headings, subheadings, indented paragraphs, and bullets.

Focus on your writing as you continue to put new skills into practice and refine your style, but don't forget the importance of white space—whether on paper or online—which will make your text more inviting to the reader.

Glossary of Idioms

above-and-beyond	more than is necessary to do the job well	ack.
all your ducks in a row	to be prepared; everything is in order	p. 83
at sea	lost, confused, "ungrounded" as if floating at sea	intro
back burner	cooking reference; not a top priority; something to do when more important tasks are completed	p. 83
(the) ball is in your court	tennis reference; the next move is up to you	p. 83
big picture	a broad overview of the subject	p. 3
bottom line	the end result—In a financial balance sheet, the final total is the bottom line.	p. 5
break even	to not come out ahead, but not lose; to end as you began	p. 84
buck the trend	to defy the odds created by a trend	p. 84
burn out	work so hard, give so much of yourself, that you cannot do any more and may risk personal well being	p. 83
burn up	become very angry	p. 83
butter up	to try to gain approval by flattery	p. 26
can't put two and two together	can't solve a simple problem; can't see the obvious	p. 83
carry a greater burden	to do more than a reasonable fair share	p. 54
chain of command	military reference; hierarchy of authority	p. 83
change gears	automotive reference; to shift or change emphasis	p. 183

charged	conveying emotion, like an electrical charge	p. 34
clog the pipeline	to slow things down	p. 15
cross-trained	taught one another's jobs	p. 61
diamond in the rough	someone with unused potential	p. 34
dig in your heels	to behave stubbornly; to be unwilling to compromise	p. 83
double life	to have two distinctly different lives —In espionage, a *double agent*, who leads a *double life*, is a spy for both sides.	P. 147
duck	to avoid	p. 85
eagle eyes	eyes that see very clearly, more clearly than most	ack.
elastic	stretchable, flexible	P. 142
fall into	to become part of an existing group	P. 142
fall off	to slowly stop doing something; *or* a decline	p. 83
from scratch	from nothing; no head start	p. 84
gem	a gem; in this context, a valued and valuable employee	p. 34
get your act together	to get organized	p. 9
go public	to be seen by others (From stock market language—A private company goes public when it sells stock to the open market.)	p. 18
go through channels	to use an established process	p. 83
go with the flow	to take things as they come	p. 15
hallmark	a distinguishing feature; a symbol of quality	p. 26
hard	specific; factual	p. 25

hope springs eternal	Even in difficult circumstances, people hope for the best.	p. 104
hurry up and wait	haste made unnecessary because it's followed by inactivity	ack.
in the ballpark	(from baseball) in the vicinity of	p. 32
in the black	operating at a profit	p. 84
in the red	operating at a loss	p. 84
join forces	to work together	p. 84
jump start	to give a push or a start; reference comes from "jump starting" cars (with jumper cables)	p. 3
keep in line	to keep in its place, or keep as it should be	p. 89
learning curve	the time it takes someone to learn something	p. 21
loose ends	unresolved or uncompleted details	p. 54
lower the boom	to give bad news without warning	p. 26
misfits	things or people that don't fit into a particular situation or group	P. 149
miss the boat	to miss an opportunity	p. 83
muse	source of creative inspiration	p. 190
off base	to be out of touch with a goal or purpose; baseball reference	p. 83
on par with	equal to; the same as	P. 144
on target	directly on point; correct conclusion or approach	p. 83
on the ball	to be aware	p. 83
on the go	moving quickly; traveling	p. 49
on the line	at risk; exposed	p. 167

out in left field	baseball reference; to be unaware of what is happening	p. 83
pepper	to sprinkle throughout	p. 15
pet	personal favorite	P. 164
plunge into	to jump in quickly, without preparation	p. 5
pruning	trimming, as pruning bushes	p. 172
reader-friendly	easy to read	p. 30
reporter questions	the standard questions asked by reporters	p. 32
saved by the bell	boxing reference (the bell that ends the round saves the boxer from another punch); saved from an unpleasant task by interruptions	p. 83
sell like hotcakes	(_not_ like hot bread)—describing a popular item that sells quickly	175
shotgun approach	to try a lot of strategies at once and hope one works	p. 83
shy away from	to avoid	p. 85
slam dunk	basketball reference; major accomplishment; well done	p. 83
slow burn	gradually become angry	p. 83
sorely	to a great extent	p. 85
spare	to the point; without excess; cut to the bone	p. 24
spin off	a new and distinctly separate product that incorporates major components of an earlier product	170
step up to the plate	baseball reference; take your turn; do what you must	p. 83
stick your neck out	to go out of your way and take a risk	p. 84

sticky	difficult	ack.
streamline	to get rid of excess	p. 77
stick with it	don't give up; continue to the end	p. 84
take root	to be solid; to develop a strong position	p. 22
three-pronged approach	an approach with three elements, or directions	p. 84
three strikes	baseball reference; you've made three mistakes and you don't get another chance	p. 83
thumbnail	a small presentation of a larger graphic or page (helpful in design and layout)	p. 189
tightly written	written with no excess words	p. 28
too much on your plate	too much to do at one time; too busy	p. 83
touch base	to get in touch with; to communicate	p. 55
tread lightly	to be careful	p. 167
(the) whole story	everything you need to know; all the facts	p. 168
wrap up	to bring to a conclusion	p. 184

◉   ◉   ◉

www.ingramcontent.com/pod-product-compliance
Lightning Source LLC
Chambersburg PA
CBHW021054090426
42738CB00006B/328